CRAVING

for

TRAVEL

CRAVING

for

TRAVEL

Luxury experiences for the sophisticated traveler

JIM STRONG CTC, ACC

Luxury Travel Books

*I dedicate this book to the man I most admire,
my father, Asa Strong*

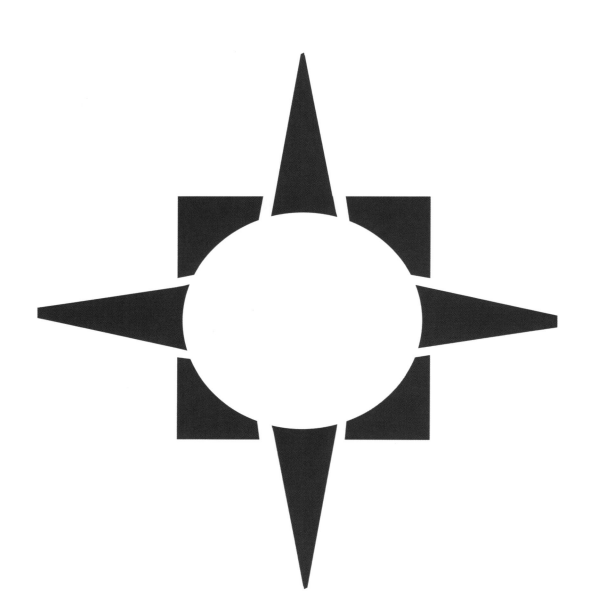

CONTENTS

Private Island Paradise

Sealed with a Kiss

The Thrill of It

Sand Between Your Toes

City-Scapes

Villa Life

Remote Hideaways

The High Seas

Sleeping Above the Clouds

INTRODUCTION

Imagine enjoying a vintage wine from the terrace of your suite with a 360 degree view of Paris and the Eiffel Tower twinkling in the background.

Imagine entertaining 20 friends at a beachfront mansion with a staff of ten at your beck and call.

Imagine yourself seated in an open Land Rover, 15 feet from a pride of lions stalking their prey.

These imaginings begin with an appetite for life—a Craving for Travel. I created this book because, as a Luxury Travel Consultant, I can bring you to the farthest reaches of the earth—and to the absolute heights of luxury. Travel is my passion and my profession. More than that, it is in my blood.

In my family, the desire to travel is so strong that we say we have an extra gene, the travel gene. It has led me across the globe in an unending search for the most unique, exotic and stylish destinations. Today I am driven by the same passion for travel that I found so powerful the first time I saw wildlife on safari; had a staff of 12 fulfill my family's every whim in our private beachfront villa; or picked fresh fruit from treetops as I reached out from the basket of a hot air balloon. Having been exposed to such life experiences—and there are more than I have room to recount here—my drive to bring meaningful events into the lives of others has continuously grown. Travel is more than a mere stamp in your passport; it leaves a lasting mark on your soul.

I believe that, though the trip ends, the experience of travel stays with you for a lifetime. Travel isn't simply recreation—it is a powerful force that transforms you and the way you see our world. It teaches us that natural beauty transcends borders and that every culture and destination lets us discover something new about ourselves and the planet that we share.

Wanderlust should know no limits. So I have spent a significant amount of time over the years visiting many destinations—places that most people do not even know exist. I have built long-standing relationships with hotel owners, managers and staff as well as concierges, drivers and guides. These connections open doors for my clients, allowing them discreet "insider" advantages.

As a professional, I do not "stay" in a hotel as you might: I quiz the staff, inspect every room type in the establishment and tug at the bed linens until I discover their label. I scrutinize every imaginable detail about the hotel but most importantly, I discover the personality of the surroundings. I'm demanding for a good reason: I am considering sending you there.

So, no surprise, my clients have come to rely on my experience and counsel when it comes to travel. They know very well that I tailor my advice and planning to them as individuals—to their personalities, their tastes, their lifestyles and, most of all, their styles of travel—in the same way a personal attorney, accountant or designer would.

While travel expertise and first-hand knowledge is essential to my business, in my view that is only part of the task. Interpretation is just as essential because travelers find far more enrichment in an orchestrated series of experiences that enhance their lives. This skill, as a seasoned professional counselor, holds a significant value to clients and is rewarded not only by financial compensation but in personal satisfaction. This recompense also clarifies my agenda; my staff and I are first and foremost your ally and your advocate.

The Internet has brought measurable change to the travel industry, but I do not see that as a threat to what I provide in the marketplace. The Internet has merely passed the labor of search and processing to the consumer without providing enough expertise or personal context to ensure the successful, rewarding trip that discerning travelers deserve. Instead, I use the Internet as an adjunct to personal service, which is indeed its greatest strength. I invite you to visit www.cravingfortravel.com, a website that complements my services and company, Strong Travel Services, Inc.

In the travel industry, such standards—and this might surprise you—are not the norm. There are roughly 25,000 travel agencies in the United States, yet only a handful approach customers as we do. It's our work to provide you with some of the highlights of your life, free of logistical details that might dampen your enjoyment of those pinnacle experiences. My customers, many of whom are CEOs and eminent leaders of society, who appreciate the luxuries of fine dining or high fashion—or who simply put a premium on how they spend their time—recognize the importance of this difference.

At Strong Travel, we routinely manage details such as chartering aircraft and private yachts. We are adept at securing personal butlers, housekeepers, gourmet chefs, nannies, cooking or wine classes, expert guides, entrée into private collections of art or the latest haute couture—and, of course, making unique requests and the one-of-a-kind marriage proposal a reality. Wherever you travel, we are there with you. Whatever you crave, we put it within reach.

More than other travel industry professionals, my staff and I have the capability to elevate our travelers to VIP status. This brings to mind what a colleague and friend says to people who consider self-service or Internet usage instead of a professional travel consultant: "You cannot 'VIP' yourself." Indeed, it takes a personal recommendation from someone who has well-established credentials and is well-known. After all, where my staff and I know the hotel manager personally and have already sent scores of sophisticated clients, you can only benefit.

Since my reputation for high standards accompanies my customers, they effortlessly reap the rewards of full red carpet treatment. But while my company may enjoy such friendly relationships around the world, we are by no means "easy" on hotels and resorts, cruise lines and airlines, or even on the governing officials of foreign destinations.

In my quest to provide the highest quality travel, I am often invited to industry meetings with other leading professionals who plan the future of travel, the building of infrastructure and the marketing of services to sophisticated travelers. These are opportunities to share my knowledge and leadership, not for public praise but to be a part of the travel industry vanguard. I am also a member of Virtuoso, a select network that invites less than 1% of professional travel consultants to join. Virtuoso's vision has helped to create inroads for luxury travelers around the world, and to advance the level of expertise among consultants. I consider these colleagues and friends part of a personal global network that ultimately benefits you, the traveler.

Strong Travel Services, Inc., began simply enough, from the desire my mother, Nancy A. Strong, CTC*, possessed for travel. Early on, she set the standard for what it means to be a leading company that provides life experiences for travelers. In 2000, she was recognized as "Travel Agent of the Year" by the American Society of Travel Agents and is repeatedly honored as one of *Travel Agent* magazine's "Most Powerful Women in Travel." *Travel + Leisure* has called her an "A-List Super Agent" year after year on their annual list of best-in-the-world travel consultants. She has served on numerous advisory boards and committees, including United Airlines, Ritz-Carlton Hotels, Starwood Luxury Hotels, Abercrombie & Kent, Rail Europe and *Travel + Leisure* magazine.

"Having raised a large family of five boys," she once recalled, "I understood about caring for people, and each time I sent someone off it was like sending off my own children." From her flair for personalized attention and the word-of-mouth that brought legions to our doors, Strong Travel grew beyond all expectations. Nancy Strong is nothing if not a role model.

She did this in no small part with the early encouragement of my father, Asa Strong, a financial business executive who is the source of strength in the Strong family. Years ago he taught my mother the monetary underpinnings of commerce as only a financial expert can. He is the reason my four brothers and I share a solid respect for discipline, organization, logic and the constant pursuit of progress in our professional lives. Those who know him may see my father as a quiet man, often absorbed in a current novel or crossword puzzle; they do not know how loudly his support speaks to us and has always spoken to us throughout the years. In his spare time, he continues to provide advice and counsel to Strong Travel.

It is evident from my parents' story, from my own experiences, from our www.cravingfortravel.com website and from this book that we view travel as no mere hobby. I am privileged to have entrée well beyond the norm all over the world and to serve an A-list of luxury seekers and connoisseurs of sophisticated style, who generously refer their friends and associates to me. Our mission is to do more than provide elite travel; it is to create trips that yield lasting memories and transformative experiences that enhance your life and style. And so have we done for the past 30 years.

No one who enjoys success does so alone. At Strong Travel, we are fortunate to have an expert and dedicated staff that stays with us year after year. I make it a point to keep them traveling so we collectively maintain a fresh and detailed worldwide expertise. I am proud of them for their constant pursuit of knowledge, tireless dedication, earnest ethical standards and genuine concern for our clients. As the face of this organization, I enjoy a national and international reputation that is in fact a reflection of the business we have all built together.

At Strong Travel, it is our priority and desire to show you the world. But, first, let us whet your appetite. The destinations that follow come with a warning: they will inspire wanderlust. So explore these pages, let your imagination wander…and see where your Craving for Travel takes you.

—*Jim Strong, CTC, ACC**
info@cravingfortravel.com

*CTC, Certified Travel Consultant, awarded by the Travel Institute

*ACC, Accredited Cruise Consultant, awarded by Cruise Lines International Association

"*...like being stranded on a desert island—from which you'll never want to be rescued.*"

Private Island Paradise

Warm sun, white sand and aquamarine ocean—the irresistible cocktail of island life! Soak up the seclusion in suites built into cliffsides or in luxury huts that stand on stilts in the middle of the sea. Privacy is redefined on a remote island rented all to yourself or with room service brought out by skiff boats. Where cares are lost, paradise is found.

Necker Island

Why buy when you can rent?—an entire island, that is.

Necker, part of the British Virgin Islands, is appropriately owned by Virgin entrepreneur Sir Richard Branson. But he's willing to rent it out to truly make this vacation your own. Consider it a way of subletting paradise.

The highlights of this island are its accommodations—with structures brought directly from Bali.

Bali Cliff is nestled on the edge of an island cliff, about 35 feet above the ocean. A resplendent hide-away, it offers a unique open-air bathroom, 280° degrees of which are completely exposed to the ocean while your modesty is kept intact.

Bali Hi is a secluded three-story house; the entire ground floor is an area to accommodate guests' new favorite pastime—lounging. A plunge pool is right outside, waiting for waterbabies and sun worshippers alike.

Bali Lo has its own freshwater pool and outdoor lounge area, complete with refrigerator for poolside refreshments and daybed for afternoon sleep in the shade. Its interior is also welcoming with exceptional island décor.

Necker Island has a striking staff delivering superb service and creative cuisine. Custom-prepared meals can be enjoyed in the chic but casual dining rooms, poolside or even on the beach. The presentation is exquisite but only hints at the unparalleled taste and freshness of the seafood.

Of course, water sports of all kinds are available here, but the snorkeling is especially fascinating with the beautiful array of aquatic life found near the island. On-land, the Bali Leha spa is Necker's answer to nirvana. It's built into the side of a cliff, offering spectacular views to those few who don't doze off during the massage.

For a wilder experience on this untamed island, book a room during Celebration Week when crowds come to enjoy Calypso bands and casino nights.

Necker Island is one of the most seductive places on earth, with soaring cliffs and pristine sand. Have the island to yourself and learn what "getting away from it all" really means.

Soneva Gili

Staying at Soneva Gili is like being stranded on a deserted island—from which you'll never want to be rescued.

In the world's premier over-water resort, Soneva Gili's Crusoe Villas are accessible only by individual dinghies. They are completely cut off from civilization, yet contain the most civilized amenities—and the luxury of uninterrupted relaxation.

The thatched hut villas are supported on stilts in the midst of a Tiffany-blue lagoon. They are built with rooftop sundecks and open-air showers screened for privacy, though there is no one else around. The verandah winds around the structure, allowing unimpeded views of the endless horizon, and steps in the bathroom lead into a private, self-contained swimming hole as the lagoon is incorporated into the architecture.

The interior hard-wood floors have glass panes cut out for viewing ocean life; suddenly, the room's large-screen TVs don't seem so appealing since high-definition can't compare to what you see beneath your feet. Sinks are made from hand-beaten silver bowls and the furniture from bleached wood, integrating design with the island's natural beauty. The whole structure is lit from within by warm lighting and tea candles, giving it a sun-on-water glow long after evening falls.

If you could bring only one thing to a deserted island, what would it be? If an espresso maker or iPod was the answer, don't bother packing. They're already provided in-room.

There are only seven of these secluded residences which represent the ultimate in isolation and all-aspects of service. Staff will row out for any request, from fresh fruit to chilled champagne, or will bring guests ashore to the Six Sense Spa for an energizing, organic anti-jet lag treatment at their glass-floored facility. Even on dry land, visitors are totally immersed in their surroundings.

Villa guests can call for room service to arrive anytime with an exotically-inspired gourmet meal—specially delivered by speed boat. But there are some good reasons to venture out of your private paradise. Paddle to shore for an on-the-beach massage. Take lunch in the over-water bar with cooked-to-order food stations or enjoy a table d'hôte dinner at the restaurant on Soneva Gili, whose menu is as ever-changing as its sunset views.

Guests can row out to a sandbar in the middle of the ocean where weekly "knee-deep" cocktail parties are held and a particularly appealing hammock is housed. Or visit a small, neighboring island containing only a single palm tree, a symbol of understated, unadulterated grace—like the Soneva Gili resort itself.

Parrot Cay

A secret escape—just a short flight from Miami.

Parrot Cay is one of the most overlooked destinations in the Caribbean-and loyal visitors hope it remains that way. After landing, a 35-minute boat ride brings guests to their exclusive villas, secluded from the outside world yet submerged in a realm of unsurpassed-and largely unexplored-beauty.

In addition to white sand beaches and unspoiled waters, this sanctuary is home to cactus groves, mangroves and marshy wetlands, lending it an untamed, otherworldly feel. But the resort's impeccable service and top-notch amenities are the height of cosmopolitan sophistication.

Beyond a natural strand of beach, the Rocky Point Villas stand as testaments to the design vision of Parrot Cay's owner, Mrs. Ong. These three-bedroom structures incorporate a clean, uncluttered aesthetic that both reflects and refines the island's environment. The spacious accommodations offer a sitting room with sweeping views and a private heated swimming pool with infinity edges that give it the illusion of stretching to the horizon.

The villas are a five-minute buggy ride from the main resort, making them the most private residences in Parrot Cay. And they come complete with personalized butler services so guests never feel too far away from the finer points of civilization.

Ocean-front beach houses and villas have private, heated pools and sundecks just outside of their whitewashed, neocolonial interiors. The canopied beds and crisp, white linens echo the simplicity and splendor of island life, which extends to the outside shower gardens. It's impossible to tell where the outdoors end and the accommodations begin.

Parrot Cay's Shambhala Spa takes a holistic approach to its services. The over-water spa area allows visitors to luxuriate in the expansive scenery while undergoing hand-picked therapeutic treatments from around the world, including an extensive selection of massages, ancient ayurverdic therapies and skin care developed exclusively for this resort. It also offers Japanese baths and an outdoor Jacuzzi garden for smaller, intimate settings that contrast the unending, panoramic ocean.

While all water sports are possible on Parrot Cay, the resort specializes in chartered bonefishing trips and island-hopping excursions for full-course golf or to nearby Iguana and Sand Dollar Islands whose names say it all.

After a day trip or activity, the resort's Asian-fusion, poolside restaurant Lotus is the definitive destination. Head chef Tippy Heng unites his Chinese-Thai heritage with Australian influences for unparalleled and unexpected cuisine, such as his signature Two-Way Tuna which combines simple ingredients in layers of flavorful complexity.

From its unmatched environment to its cuisine and accommodations, Parrot Cay turns uncomplicated living into an exquisite art. The simple life never seemed so good.

North Island

A sanctuary for guests—and Nature.

North Island is located between India and Africa, in one of the world's most pristine ecosystems. In order to preserve that, the resort runs on a philosophy of natural regeneration and protection of indigenous wildlife, which is spectacularly abundant. Guests are incorporated into a lifestyle that celebrates nature and barefoot luxury.

The design concept for the accommodations utilizes local materials, such as the large Takamaka trees which died of natural causes and had to be removed from the ground. They were used to create the resort's dining room and other furnishings in the villas, keeping the architectural motif in line with the natural splendor of the island.

There are eleven private bungalows, each with an attention to detail that demonstrates the confluence of natural elements and man-made structures. One villa includes a bridge carved from two island trees leading to the bedroom suite. A sunken stone bathtub has delicately sloped natural edges to cradle a bottle of champagne. And an outdoor shower receives water through a hollowed-out log that diverts run-off from a large granite boulder; the shower curtain is made from tiny pieces of coral collected from the beach. The design is a perfect mixture of earthly elements and architectural inspiration.

Guests' enjoyment of their natural surroundings is completely unobstructed. Large palms frame ocean views; villas soar above the sea, perched on magnificent rocks; bedrooms include removable glass doors to allow free reign to ocean breezes and the public lounge is a transparent building that doesn't block breathtaking views.

The dining room at North Island is set against granite rock with a small pond issuing

out onto a deck, blurring the boundaries between natural and formal settings. The cuisine makes use of the island's prodigious resources (as does the spa), spicing up seafood and local vegetation with a Southeast Asian flair.

Perhaps the best part of North Island is the limitless activities it offers. Its dive center offers excursions into some of the most spectacular diving sites in the world, including Shark Bank, which guarantees some exciting underwater sightings.

The staff at North Island participates in nurturing the island's sea turtle population and, depending on the time of year, guests may witness the birthing and nesting of the young. A boat trip to Silhouette Island introduces visitors to an ecology center that houses endangered giant tortoises. These are activities designed not only to amuse but to enlighten.

The layout of the North Island resort is intended to resemble a small, primitive island village with historical layerings and roots that reach down into the land. Instead of entering pre-fabricated structures designed along the latest trends, guests enter a part of the island's history and culture-and leave better off for the experience.

Lizard Island

There are twenty-four white sand beaches on Lizard Island, like singular hours of a perfect day.

Lizard Island is found off Australia, on the inner side of the Great Barrier Reef. This distinctive location gives guests an insider's look at 400 acres of national parkland, replete with rolling hills, granite cliffs, dozens of secluded coves and coral reefs alive with marine life. So while the beaches certainly are tempting, traveling here is not simply limited to lying on the sand—though it is advisable for at least one day. In true Australian spirit, adventure abounds.

Plenty of activities are offered on Lizard Island, from the requisite snorkeling to catamarans, glass-bottomed boats and night diving. On dry land, guests can partake in nature walks, following private paths that lead from the suites to secluded relaxation areas, or bring along a gourmet picnic hamper-packed by the hotel staff-for an evening outing on the beach.

In-room amenities are also geared to get guests outdoors. Accommodations at the Pavilion, perched high above the Coral Sea at the edge of Sunset Ridge, include private plunge pools, sun lounges and outside daybeds-forgoing television sets and radios for ocean views and the sound of crashing waves. High-powered binoculars in one hand allow for wildlife viewing as guests stake out some of the island's namesakes…while the other hand is occupied with a glass of complimentary Bollinger champagne.

The Sunset Point Villas are also set high on the ridge among eucalyptus bushland with easy access to a string of secluded beaches. The outdoor deck is complete with a hammock that's guaranteed not to stay empty for long.

Anchor Bay Suites are set in a sweeping arc along the untamed beauty of the bay that just begs to be explored. Rooms are located in a tropical garden setting with easy access to both the bay and beach-and to the hammock on their private balconies.

The Azure Spa uses local marine ingredients in its signature treatments, such as the Coral Sea Dreaming facial and massage or the Mermaid's Secret body wrap and polish. These luxuries leave guests looking as resplendent and naturally beautiful as their surroundings.

The tropical setting of Lizard Island is reflected in its cuisine, which emphasizes fresh seafood, local produce and lush tropical fruits prepared in diverse ways to showcase the multitude of cultural influences converging in Australia. The resort's tiki-themed lounge is comprehensively stocked with quality beer, wine and spirits and it's always open so drop by after quenching your thirst for adventure.

With an average year-round temperature of 81°F (warmer in winter), Lizard Island presents the richness of life fully realized-and waiting just outside your door.

"*…here where you'll most likely discover a lost treasure—the ability to savor the richness of each moment.*"

Sealed with a Kiss

Some destinations are designed for romance—cliffside settings above the Amalfi Coast and the Côte d'Azur that leave you breathless; the quiet charms of the Italian countryside, French vineyards and Vermont woodlands that transport you to other worlds and times; the allure of Hollywood and the sultriness of the American Southwest that seep into your skin; luxury resorts that reaffirm love at first sight.

Hotel Bel-Air

Arriving at the Hotel Bel-Air is like putting on a favorite pair of designer jeans—guests feel comfortable, chic and are suddenly the center of attention.

Located in Los Angeles, the Mission-style hotel has pink stucco, lush greens, spraying fountains and soaring palm trees that give it an undeniable Hollywood style. To add to the fantasy, guests enter this setting across a canopied stone bridge over Swan Lake.

Red carpet treatment is an everyday occurrence at Hotel Bel-Air. The level of personal attention guests receive is remarkable, with a three-to-one staff-to-guest ratio. Casually mention your favorite flowers then be amazed by a bouquet of them in your room. Enjoy a lovely afternoon tea presented en suite upon your arrival or request preparation of your private fireplace at any time. The beauty is in the details.

The service at this hotel is sterling because they've had years of practice perfecting it on celebrities such as Cary Grant, who favored the dark, cozy bar next to the dining room, and Marilyn Monroe, who shared a cottage with her husband Joe DiMaggio and for whom the fitness center is appropriately named. Rich in Hollywood history, the Hotel Bel-Air is a modern take on the glamorous, golden days of cinema.

The ninety-one guest rooms at Hotel Bel-Air, each with private entrance, are distinctively designed and can be custom-decorated upon request for longer stays. No two are exactly alike and some include touches, like outdoor terrace Jacuzzis, that really set them apart.

The Swan Lake Suite is one of the most celebrated. Its only entrance is through a white picket fence to give it a storybook setting, with views of fountain courtyards and flowering bird-of-paradise trees. The formal living room was created by elite designers from the finest materials imaginable.

Naturally, like its namesake, the Grace Kelly Suite is perhaps the most elegant room offered at the hotel. Shades of crimson decorate the walls and floor-to-ceiling picture windows look out onto lavish landscapes and a romantic fountain. It's the kind of setting most people think exists only in movies.

The Herb Garden Suite offers the most privacy, with a large bedroom, library, adjoining reading area, dining room and private kitchen-plus staff who will come to prepare

your meals. Its two huge baths and formal living room with hand-painted murals on the ceiling are favorites among returning guests. There are few reasons ever to want to leave this suite...except for that California sun calling from the outdoor terrace.

Boredom is never an issue while staying at the Hotel Bel-Air. Besides its LA location, there are in-house amenities that keep guests entertained. The pool is a favorite spot for celebrity sunbathers and is always heated at an ideal 82°F.

The Wine Terrace, one of the hotel's hottest attractions, hosts over forty wine and food events per year. Able to accommodate private parties of up to twenty, it's the ideal spot for an upscale occasion or a special intimate gathering.

The hotel's Terrace Restaurant was voted one of the Most Romantic Hotel Restaurants, a perfect place to woo your significant other. Every detail breathes quality, from the French-California cuisine to the tablecloths hand-woven by Italian nuns.

It takes a lot to impress the people of Los Angeles but in a city that has it all, nothing outshines the Hotel Bel-Air.

Le Toiny

There are two treasures to be found on St. Bart's: One belonged to a buccaneer and is believed to be buried somewhere on the island; the other is Hotel Le Toiny.

This quiet villa resort rests on a hillside on the southeastern coast of St. Barthélemy, in a yet undeveloped area, surrounded by rare trees and cacti overlooking a lagoon. This setting looks much the same today as when Columbus first discovered it in 1493 and, so impressed by its natural splendor, named it after his brother Bartolomeo.

St. Bart's wild beauty went largely uninhabited until French colonists from Normandy and Brittany settled there 150 years later, accounting for its still-evident taste of Continental cool in the midst of the sweltering Caribbean. French pirates swarmed here, bringing with them items of prosperity plundered from Spanish galleons. Who knows what you'll discover digging your toes in the sand?

Even if the search for gold doubloons comes up empty, there are plenty of riches to be found at the Hotel Le Toiny, from its neighboring bird refuge to the internationally-acclaimed cuisine at Le Gaiac French restaurant and the generously proportioned cottages, each designed to let in abundant amounts of natural light. There is no better way to wake up than to birdsong and bright sun.

The hotel's tin-roofed Antillean cottages are staggered for optimal privacy and airy ocean views. They are furnished in unassuming neocolonial elegance and French toile, and include sunken sundecks, private pools and capacious four-poster beds that appear to float above the floor, as the legs are hidden by diaphanous drapings. The sensation is one of sleeping atop the ocean, lulled by gentle breezes.

The main cottage is a lavish compound secreted behind an old-fashioned swinging gate and flanked by lush gardens and rare blue flowered Gaiac trees, known as the Trees of Life. Its rooms are orchestrated with high ceilings, polished mahogany and sprays of fresh flowers—neocolonial settings out of Hemingway stories.

The hotel's hospitality begins before guests even reach their rooms. One of Le Toiny's chauffeurs greets visitors at the airport and escorts them to their cottage, where Rosé Champagne will already be chilled and a gourmet plate awaits. To pursue personal adventures, a soft-top Jeep is delivered to your door for use throughout your stay.

Cuisine is an essential part of island life that often replaces other organized activities. An evening tête-a-tête is transformed into an event in itself, as coffee, night caps and light fare are served with soft musical selections and an accompaniment of cicadas and chirping tree frogs. There are about sixty restaurants on the island, where dining has been elevated to a grand art and wine cellars are always well-stocked—though breakfast is cordially served every morning next to your private pool.

Of course, island life always revolves around the ocean and, at St. Bart's, surfing is so popular that championship contests are held every month. In addition, yearly events such as the St. Bart's Regatta and Cup may inspire guests to charter their own 20-meter yacht for a full day's sail.

The Hotel Le Toiny's reception desk arranges a variety of pastimes, from excursions to the nearby island of St. Kitts to duty-free shopping trips, where expensive name brands sit alongside delicately woven straw work braided by the expert hands of villagers. Perhaps the best way to immerse yourself in island culture is a trip to the main port of Gustavia, where sailors, boat hands and locals gather at dusk for dominoes and beer. The atmosphere is both languorous and vibrant and it is here that you'll most likely discover a lost treasure—the ability to savor the richness of each moment.

Grand Hotel a Villa Feltrinelli

A shimmering image of Old World charm is reflected in one of Italy's most beautiful bodies of water.

Though relatively small, the magnificent Villa Feltrinelli is among the finest residences in the country, with immense amenities and a one-of-a-kind history.

The 1892 Liberty-style mansion belonged to the Feltrinelli family, who owned a publishing company and a lumber empire that stretched throughout Europe-accounting for the villa's ornate, highly-glossed woodwork. The hotel's décor recaptures the ambience of a summer home owned by a privileged Italian family with a penchant for travel and discovery. It invites guests to experience the same.

The Villa rests on the shore of Lake Garda, a beautiful body of water framed by a backdrop of mountains. Italians have a way of making the most stunning natural settings even more attractive through their use of architecture, and Villa Feltrinelli is no exception. It stands as a centerpiece amidst formal landscapes with century-old trees, olive groves and a tiered lemon garden-a crowning achievement of structural design and Art Nouveau accents with the unimposing feel of a country villa.

Familial touches lend Villa Feltrinelli a warm, lived-in charm. A pantry stocked with snacks and beverages is kept open 24 hours for guests to raid as they wish—it's especially popular around midnight. An exquisite Bösendorfer piano graces the lobby and is frequently used for early evening classical concertos, reminiscent of family life at the turn of the century. The dining area is an intimate masterpiece, with walls dressed in hand-painted fabrics and up to fourteen guests seated around the Feltrinelli's original table, sharing a supper of freshly-made pasta.

The Villa is steeped in quiet luxury. For evenings in, there's an octagonal card room furnished with Chesterfield loveseats and cocktails served in vintage Italian glasses unearthed at a local market. Hand-carved sitting benches adorn the entryway like the fine wooden pews of a cathedral. The villa's priceless frescoes were restored to original grandeur by local graduates of Italy's premiere art schools as a labor of love. It is from such elements that Villa Feltrinelli resonates with a serene beauty born of deep attachment to the country, its culture and citizens.

Entering the guest rooms produces a feeling of homecoming. The hotel offers 21 rooms and suites, each individually decorated and so exquisitely detailed as to seem customized to their current occupants. The 7 guest rooms in the main villa feature fresco ceilings hand-

painted in the 1890s by the Lieti brothers and incorporate 70 pieces of original antique furniture that came with the estate. "Il Poeta" is a study in understated grace, with lovely star-shaped windows overlooking Lake Garda. "Al Lago" houses bedroom pieces once used by Mussolini on this estate, his final dwelling place.

Personal flourishes elevate the Casa Rustica guest house to a level of eminence. Hand-crafted Venetian lamps are set upon bedside tables; embossed sheets are 100% Egyptian cotton and a discreetly concealed high-fidelity stereo offers a quality selection of opera and jazz CDs, culled from the owner's own prodigious collection. Each room is a litany of fine detail and infinite care.

Attention to guests' needs extends even to the bathrooms, with heated marble floors and oversized "deluge" showerheads. "Il Poeta's" French cast-iron, triple-porcelain bathtub is secluded behind an elegant oak-paneled partition, set amid warm white finishings and deep, rich woodwork-a tableau of clean-lined elegance overlooking the calm waters of Lake Garda.

Near the Boat House, a lovely residence with fireplace and outdoor terrace set along the lake shore, guests can avail themselves of The Contessa, the Villa's private boat. This 16-meter craft, commissioned in a local boatyard and patterned after a 1920s American river boat, glides on sun-drenched waters, taking guests to lakeside restaurants and affording spectacular views of the Villa illuminated along the shoreline.

In all regards, Villa Feltrinelli is a portrait of restrained opulence, like a well-metered line in a verse of rare beauty. Its hospitality and polish are symbols of another era, passed on through the ancestral soil of a summer manor.

Twin Farms

Sometimes a simple walk in the woods leads to paths of undiscovered wonder.

Start your journey just 1½ miles east of the general store at Twin Farms in Vermont. This 235-acre estate situated in secluded woodlands was novelist Sinclair Lewis' wedding present to his wife. A romantic inn set amid apple orchards with a dramatic backdrop of mountain ranges, Twin Farms is a year-round retreat of rustic luxury.

The accommodations at Twin Farms are built around individual themes, giving each one the feel of a private mountain hideaway. Rooms in the Main House include Mr. Lewis' master bedroom, featuring a blue slate fireplace, décor fashioned around a needlepoint rug and an antique clawfoot bathtub. An adjoining room has been redone as a French chateau, adorned with festive green toile that depicts Marquis de Lafayette's arrival on the new continent. It includes a walk-through dressing room and overlooks tiered gardens that send refreshing fragrances through wide open windows.

Also of note are the nine separate cottages, each of distinct character. The Chalet resembles a Swiss structure, with soaring spaces and a comfortable interior that manages to seem both lived-in and untouched. The centerpiece of the Chalet is a rare blue marble fireplace that adds a warm intimacy to the high-ceilinged, sunken living room. Infinity decks look out onto views that span for 30 miles and the screened porch is the perfect spot for morning coffee.

The Tree House bares little resemblance to those built in youth. This sophisticated interpretation is set amidst a pine wood and includes accents of white birch beams and a four-poster bed with wrought-iron bird sculptures perched atop each post. The en suite steam shower is an ideal way to relax in a most tranquil setting.

The Log Cabin's unassuming exterior belies the uniqueness of its river rock fireplace and the fine detail of its sturdy, hand-built furniture. The Woods Cottage, surrounded by spruce and cherry trees, has an outdoor fireplace, indoor trees encircling a soaking tub and a split log staircase leading to a reading loft.

Each accommodation has an easy, straightforward charm with layers of unobtrusive finery: Hockney and Lichtenstein's original paintings hung with casual flair, beams polished to a high shine, chandeliers made unexpectedly lovelier with the weight of wrought iron. These sturdy, thought-out details add up to an ambience of substantial beauty.

Restrained elegance continues into the shared spaces. The always-open, self-serve bar is referred to simply as The Pub, with the warm atmosphere of a favorite local hangout—albeit worlds away. Its main features are an inviting billiards table, a Wurlitzer jukebox and a Steinway grand, all bathed in the glow of an antler chandelier.

Hardy meals prepared with ingredients from Twin Farms' own organic vegetable and herb gardens or plates of Vermont cheese can

be enjoyed in front of The Pub's large-screen TVs, taken leisurely on cottage porches or carried along in a backpack on a scenic hike. The imaginative cuisine superbly reflects the changing seasons and incorporates wholesome takes on continental comfort food.

A walk through the surrounding acreage stretches past perennial gardens and ponds or across a covered bridge with nearby waterfalls. In summer, this setting is ideal for fly-fishing or canoeing; sunset meals of champagne and lobster can be savored in the solitude of a canoe in the middle of a tranquil lake. In winter, skiing and ice-skating are supplemented by scenic sleigh rides with warm mugs of cider.

The estate also provides guests with mountain bikes for long, leisurely autumnal rides (and complimentary return pick-up service if the foliage entices you too far), low-key cocktail hours held in the cozy and immaculate barn and an indoor Japanese hot bath to soak away any slight soreness from unending afternoons spent in the outdoors.

Twin Farms elevates simple living, finding splendid details within a world of immense beauty.

Chateau de Bagnols

In the heart of the Beaujolais vineyards and the hills of the Lyonnais, the Château de Bagnols stands as a stately symbol of French history and aristocracy.

Though "discreet" rarely describes an eight-century old castle, this gracious country residence commands a quiet grandeur, secure of its resounding place in history. The structure was originally built to rival the imposing estates of royalty and clergy, and the classical design and lush manicured lawns certainly bring to mind images of Versailles. Yet the current owner, Lady Hamlyn, added touches of warmth and whimsical décor that make the Château's austere beauty accessible.

The Château's sterling lineage can be traced through its dramatic architecture. The drawbridge, moat, medieval towers and fortifications reveal its 13th-century origins; harmonious courtyards, classical proportions and exquisite wall paintings are a legacy from the Renaissance; and a visit from King Charles VIII is commemorated with a crown carved into the original stone fireplace. The building is situated in the country's Golden Stone region, accounting for the exterior's honey-colored hue.

Accommodations are fittingly spectacular and are either part of the main building or in the restored stables beside the inner courtyard. The most requested room is the lit à la Polonaise with its antique draperies of yellow silk, harkening back to the heyday of Lyon's silk-weaving industry, and the 18th-century grisaille detailing above a stone fireplace.

Another suite set in a charming alcove incorporates golden 17th-century rococo bedposts and wall paintings that depict the life of St. Jèrôme. Each suite is named for a famous personage who is somehow historically linked to the building and pieces of museum-quality antique furniture recreate an atmosphere of the Château's original splendor.

Entering any room is like stepping into a self-contained work of art. A Pompeiian bathroom-voted the most beautiful in the world-is a tableau of perfect symmetry and uncluttered sumptuousness. The main dining room is bedecked with ornate candelabras and a wall-length Gothic fireplace, a spectacle enhanced by serenading opera singers and piano concertos.

The grand showpiece of the Château de Bagnols is the cuvage-a huge room of stone vaulted ceilings and exposed beams that houses several 17th-century wine presses and barrels, vestiges of the estate's enduring ties to the local vineyards.

Located in the center of fine French cooking, the Château boasts high culinary standards and dishes transformed into the stuff of legends-with seasonal ingredients culled from the grounds' own vegetable gardens and complemented by specially commissioned Limoge china. Many guests leave the Château feeling that they've had their finest meal.

A few steps from the sculptured, Louis VIX-style gardens rests the Salon d'Ombrage, where a table is laid out in the shade of ancient lime trees near a terrace of lavender. Gourmet meals can be taken anywhere on the picturesque grounds, which are dotted with half-buried huts once used to store ice brought by ship from Scandinavia.

Many of the activities offered by the estate take place on or near the lawns. A private wine-tasting is held one kilometer away in the old cellar of Count Claude de Rambuteau. The Chateau's executive chef offers cooking classes for guests to refine their techniques in the French tradition. A heated Roman swimming pool overlooks a scenic hillside town. Horse carriage rides and cycling take guests past ancient stone architecture and perfumed flower fields.

For an experience that cannot be duplicated, hot air balloons lift off from the estate's property and glide over the region's sloping green hills and verdant vineyards. The countryside comes alive as a patchwork of rich color and texture-beautifully captured in the Château's trump l'oeil wall paintings.

A stay in the Château de Bagnols is a step back in time—in a manner befitting a member of the royal court.

Palazzo Sasso

Tucked in the hills 1,000 feet above Italy's famed Amalfi coast, the small town of Ravello is made even more glorious by the stunning architecture of Palazzo Sasso.

This modestly-sized hotel was originally built in the 12th-century as a private home, a showpiece to illustrate fortunes made through merchant trading. Like much of Ravello's oldest buildings, the Palazzo incorporates Moorish influences-pointed archways, geometrically-patterned tiled floors, grand staircases-trends of the time that reflect the riches of the far East.

Palazzo Sasso's current incarnation was overseen by local architects who visualized an intimate, small-scale structure to contrast the region's very large architectural tradition. The hotel does not force its mark on history since so much history already exists in Ravello. Instead, its dignified presence whispers from the hilltops, carried on the winds of time.

Centuries of kings, popes and English lords have been brought to Ravello by the inherent allure of the Amalfi coast. Boccaccio's 14th-century Decameron recounts a visit here to "a villa with a large and splendid courtyard" with rooms "admirable and ornate." It could well be a description of Palazzo Sasso.

More recent examples of royalty have made their way through Ravello. Greta Garbo found the privacy she sought; André Gide found inspiration in its views, writing that the town "is closer to heaven than it is to earth;" Gore Vidal, who claims to live exclusively in his mind, chose to settle down in its seclusion.

After the Palazzo reopened as a hotel in the 1950s, Ingrid Bergman, Roberto Rossellini (for whom the restaurant is named) and other film luminaries shooting in Rome came to this retreat for glamorous repose.

The hotel's design concept is grounded in local tradition, reconciled with modern sensibility. The stately suites take their cue from a wide Italian heritage, with marble from the north and color patterns that reflect the blues and yellows of sea and sun. Interior Moorish columns add a hint of the exotic and arched windows open out to an expanse of untamed coastline and the unimaginable beauty of the Mediterranean.

The Belvedere Suite is a white-washed, free-standing structure at one end of a garden terrace-the remains of a medieval defense against pirates. This private suite has a hidden entrance, tiered gardens which slope down the hillside and a rooftop sundeck from which to soak up the scenery.

The sun filters in through tall Moorish arches and lush vines growing across wooden pergolas—like those used throughout the region for growing grapes or sheltering lemon

trees. The Belvedere's bedroom was placed on a slightly higher plane than the sitting room so unobstructed views of the Mediterranean can be seen from bed immediately upon waking.

Palazzo Sasso's grounds are a gorgeous display of design and texture. The swimming pool, flanked by palm trees and stone staircases, reflects warm lights from the terrace above and resembles a simple garden fountain. The heated pool also features an underwater window—and looking out at the sea from this level feels like being suspended in air.

Terraced gardens provide shady walks under magnolias by day or moonlit strolls at night. Bronze statues copied from ones unearthed at Pompeii overlook latticed hills and sleepy fishing villages along the coastline.

The hotel's light-flooded entrance, with 12th-century columns supporting overhead arches, opens into an antique-filled parlor, over which portraits of Neapolitan nobility reign. A winding stairway leads to two heated Jacuzzis on the rooftop solarium.

Dinners at the hotel's Rossellinis Restaurant are so good that yachts actually change course and anchor in the bay so guests can come up for the cuisine. Since Ravello is poised between sea and mountain, nightly ingredients include freshly caught fish, cuts of meat from animals fed on figs, and wild-growing mushrooms, chestnuts and fennel. The local lemons are famous and are featured in such dishes as lemon and honey fritters with warm goat cheese from local farms.

While the regional wines are exceptional, production is small so they remain a well-kept local secret. The Palazzo's recommended wine is produced from ancient vines at nearby Pompeii, in vineyards of rich volcanic soil.

Palazzo Sasso provides unique activities that may temporarily distract guests from the sea and sun. Mamma Agata's cooking lessons take place in her private home atop a cliff, where she grows much of the food used in her special recipes. Ceramic classes are offered at a famed local factory. And Ravello is full of little paths and garden lanes that lead through the mountains to the small town of Scala or other villages so linked along the Amalfi coast.

There are also abundant opportunities for excursions or scenic drives by the seaside. The Roman ruins of Pompeii and Greek temples of Paestum are a short distance away, as are the world-renowned cities of Amalfi and Positano.

Boat trips can be taken to the island of Capri-allowing guests to admire the breathtaking landscape and stop off at small bays for a swim. Be sure to return to the hotel in time for its chic cocktail and canapés hours or for power coffee breaks with paninis and freshly baked cakes.

With such immense grandeur in a small-scale setting, the Palazzo Sasso presides like a bejeweled beacon over one of the world's most dazzling coasts.

Palazzo Sasso

Le Chateau du Domaine St. Martin

Lyrical views of the Côte d'Azur—from the heights of luxury.

La Château du Domaine St. Martin has been centuries in the making. Resting on a hillside above the French Riviera, the resort is built on the ruins of an ancient Roman fortress site, later converted into the Commanderie of the Knights of Templar, who chose the spot for its strategic location. Now coveted for its resplendent views, the Château estate is still rumored to house some of the Knights' fabled belongings.

In 350, St. Martin, the Bishop of Tours for whom the area is now named, settled on the estate—leading the way for countless other tourists to follow in his footsteps.

The Château's rich history only adds to its modern-day allure. Guests strolling the grounds come across the remnants of an ancient drawbridge. Eighteenth-century tapestries and original paintings hang in the meeting rooms and wood-paneled bar. Near the lounge's open fireplace, an archway is adorned on either side with authentic gouache medallions. Louis XV and XVI furniture complement the tasteful junior suites and the six spacious bastides (two-and-three-bedroom villas)—each with a spectacular sea view.

The Château du Domaine makes the most of its unparalleled location high above the lovely Riviera. Its fourteen hectares of gardens were designed by acclaimed landscape artist Jean Mus and include scenic relaxation areas with sweeping views of the villages and sea beneath.

Perhaps the height of sophistication is partaking in an evening aperitif on a private patio perched above the French shoreline with the lights of town shining from below.

The estate grounds are immaculately manicured for optimal enjoyment. Petanque lawns abound for afternoon amusement, followed by high tea in the lounge. An overflowing pool is the same crystalline blue as the sky, blurring the distinction between the hillside and horizon. L'Oliveraie grill is nestled among tiered olive trees and serves light Mediterranean dishes in an outdoor setting perfumed by gardens of lavender and rosemary that mingle with the food's own fresh aromas.

For a more formal setting, La Commanderie, a one-Michelin-star restaurant, serves grand cuisine in an unequalled environment—situated within the Château's corner tower. A wrap-around terrace allows for al fresco dining amongst sea breezes.

St. Martin occupies an ideal location in the South of France. Guests are never far from interesting day trips to medieval villages or shopping excursions to Vallauris for handcrafted pottery, Biot for blown glasswork, or Grasse for customized scents and perfume. Nearby museums house the great works of Chagall, Matisse, Picasso and Renoir. Or, for a chic getaway, the towns of Monaco, synonymous with the South of France, and Cannes, a cultural center for film and the arts, lie within 30 miles of the estate.

For a more convenient—and memorable—mode of travel, charter a private helicopter tour departing from the Chateau's own on-grounds heliport. The panoramic view of St. Martin from the sky seems custom-made for a hand-held camcorder; perhaps this entry will earn the prestigious Palme d'Or at next year's Cannes Film Festival.

With its compelling history and resplendent hillside location, Château du Domaine St. Martin literally soars above other resorts on the French Riviera.

"Hawking in the Perthshire hills is a sensory thrill: heather-scented air, the tinkling of soft bells, the taut grasp of talons as the hawk steadies to the hand. It is the stuff of royalty and of legend."

The Thrill of It

From helicoptering onto Rocky Mountain peaks to safaris in the African veldt to falconing in the Scottish highlands, the sport in these pleasure spots is thrilling and the thrill is always sporting. Big Cats, downhill skiing, championship golf courses—all beckon visitors seeking high adventure in the world's most superb locales.

Mala Mala

A wildlife wonderland, the Mala Mala game reserve deep within the verdant hills of the South African veldt beckons visitors to the wilderness adventure of a lifetime.

Mala Mala is an environmental sanctuary located on the Sand River that presents a vision of uniquely beautiful animals in their natural habitat, with emphasis on the Big Five: lion, leopard, rhinoceros, elephant, and buffalo. The Reserve comprises 33,000 acres of pristine game-viewing land, making it the largest privately owned game reserve in South Africa. Roaming herds of antelope, giraffe, zebra and wildebeest, along with hyena, jackal, wild dog and cheetah, add depth to the safari. Adjacent to Kruger National Park, the 19 km open border allows unimpeded access to migratory animals of every variety.

Here, the animals feel unthreatened by human presence due to stringent policies implemented to insure minimal human intrusion. Interactions that are normally seen only in television documentaries unfold before the observer's eyes.

Upon arrival guests are assigned a ranger/game expert to administer to their needs. A staff to guest ratio of 3:1 ensures that every need is met. University graduates in the natural sciences and masters of bush lore, rangers present a fascinating interpretation and history of the region and ecosystem. Together, rangers and trackers conduct photographic safaris in open 4-wheel-drive vehicles, allowing for freedom of movement and the ability to travel off road into the bush, where sightings of the Big Five are greatly increased. After dark, spotlight safaris provide the opportunity to view nocturnal creatures and carnivores on the hunt.

The Mala Mala camp atmosphere is designed to support an authentic experience and complete an African mosaic. Accommodation is in thatched units, the interiors furnished with rich wall hangings and bronze flourishes. There are eighteen rooms, including luxury suites, a suite for disabled travelers, and family rooms, accommodating up to thirty-six guests.

Amenities include his and her bathrooms

in each room, robes, hair dryers, insect-proof screening on all windows, a mini bar in every bedroom, purified water, Internet access, and, of course, air conditioning/heating twenty-four hours per day. The beautifully appointed camp features a library with satellite television, intimate safari bar, and large pool.

The lounge and dining room have a "safari" feel, featuring plush couches and chairs, and walls festooned with animal trophies, skins, and other artifacts. A large deck shaded by enormous jackal-berry trees overlooks the Sand River, where animals continually arrive to drink and bathe. This magnificent view provides a picturesque backdrop for breakfast and lunch, served beneath oversized canvas umbrellas. Dinners consisting of venison specialties and haute bush cuisine are enjoyed under the stars in the traditional African boma, to the accompaniment of the rich night sounds of the African veldt.

Finally, there is newly-built Rattray's Camp, with fifteen suites overlooking the Sand River. Plunge pools complete each of the secluded verandas, and an outdoor dining area provides the ideal vantage point from which to enjoy bush cuisine. Facilities here include a viewing deck with telescope, an air-conditioned library, and a wine cellar stocked with South Africa's best wines. (This camp has a 16-year-plus age requirement.)

A legendary and exclusive safari destination, Mala Mala, internationally recognized as the top game viewing destination in the world, presents an exhilarating and unforgettable travel experience.

The Ritz-Carlton, Bachelor Gulch

Colorado in its purest form commences at the base of Beaver Creek Mountain.

In another century, a group of bachelors hewed from the mountain a place reflecting a dream of tranquility and repose they could not find in the towns below. Today, their vision is alive at the Ritz-Carlton, Bachelor Gulch, a countrified deluxe accommodation inspired by the grand lodges of the American West.

Located in the heart of a great national forest, this lavish, all-season resort, specializing in some of the finest skiing, golfing, and dining in America, is an exquisite Rocky Mountain luxury hotel offering panoramic views of snow-capped mountains and lush forests from nearly all of its 237 guestrooms and suites.

The eleven-story rustic rock-and-log exterior is marked by steeply pitched roofs. In place of a lobby is a magnificent great room, where massive timbers and a soaring stone hearth provide mountain ambience, with leather and rich upholstered seating often taken up by the après-ski crowd.

Featuring the ultimate in high-end sports-two championship golf courses designed by pro golfers Tom Fazio and Greg Norman, and 1,625 ski-able acres containing 13 lifts and 6 high-speed quads-activities include skating and snowboarding in winter and whitewater rafting, backcountry hiking, and hot air ballooning during summer.

Boasting many uncommon conveniences, the hotel offers ski vacation service for parents. In the mornings, parents may drop children off with a Ski Nanny, who furnishes breakfast and then escorts them to ski school where they receive group lessons. She then collects them in the afternoon and conducts them to Ritz Kids Roundup, which provides a variety of creative activities for children between the ages of five and twelve.

Another unique feature of Bachelor Gulch is the Ski Concierge, who greets skiers at the bottom of the slope at day's end and collects and stores gear for the following day. The next morning everything is cleaned and awaiting pickup; as a special touch ski boots are even warm and dry.

The Loan-a-Lab program is one more original and fun-filled aspects of the Ritz-Carlton. Bachelor, the hotel's resident yellow Labrador retriever and mascot, a friendly and energetic retriever, is available to individuals or families for walks and runs. The program is by reservation Monday through Friday; Bachelor gratefully

accepts any donations in his name made to the local Humane Society.

Accommodations include Mountainside, Valleyside, and Deluxe Mountainside suites, with private balconies and window seats affording breathtaking views of Beaver Creek Mountain. Club Level suites feature two and three bedroom accommodations with fireplaces and picture windows for a tantalizing view of the Eagle River valley. The hotel also features lavish top-floor Residences containing massive two and three bedroom units. With wondrous views of what appears as the entirety of the Rocky Mountains, these units can sometimes be rented out.

Ultra-luxurious baths contain large bathtub windows for the ultimate in relaxed viewing. They also have deep tubs and stall showers, Frette linens, plush terry robes, and marble floors. Living areas are decorated with Craftsman-style lamps and snowshoes hanging on the walls; specialized accents include bright, patterned fabrics of pinecones and mountain foliage.

Emphasizing natural health, The Bachelor Gulch Spa is the last word in relaxation and rejuvenation. There is a complete fitness center; services include massage, body and facial treatments utilizing indigenous natural emollients, and, of course, classes in relaxation techniques stressing yoga and Pilates. With nineteen treatment rooms, state-of-the-art facilities include steam, sauna, and indoor/outdoor whirlpools, all highlighted by a coed rock grotto with a bubbling "lazy river" whirlpool.

Dining at Bachelor Gulch can be rated on a sliding scale ranging from the marvelous to the amazing. The signature restaurant here is Remington's, with its vaulted ceilings and

sagebrush accents, where the new Scottish-born chef embellishes the Ritz-Carlton's regional approach with a menu that offers American classics like venison, elk loin, duck, trout, and rack of lamb, as well as the very finest porterhouse and Delmonico steaks.

Outdoors, the Mountainside Terrace and Daybreak Deli provide more casual dining, with fare such as fresh-ground bison burgers; the deli features a carving board and over-stuffed sandwiches along with various beers and ales. The Fly Fishing Library is available for cocktails and light snacks, while The Private Dining Room can be reserved for intimate events with an individualized menu.

The Ritz-Carlton, Bachelor Gulch, offers the very finest in luxury-sporting vacations in a dazzling Colorado venue while capturing the spirit of the unspoiled American West.

Gleneagles

Classic in architecture and aristocratic in spirit, Gleneagles is not only an infinitely comfortable and amenable five-star Scottish hotel but also a luxury estate designed for activities springing from the Anglo-Saxon sporting tradition.

Poised on the edge of the Highlands in the White Muir of Auchterarder, Gleneagles is nestled in a violet bowl in the Ochil Hills, with a view on a clear day as far as Ben Lomond in the west and the Grampian Mountains in the north. Here rest and repose blend effortlessly with vigor and energy.

Gleneagles is synonymous with golf—it will host the Ryder Cup in 2014. The King's and Queen's courses were planned in 1919 by five-time British Open winner James Braid, who shaped them around the features and natural hazards of the countryside. In 1993, Jack Nicklaus designed the third championship course, the PGA Centenary Course, which is the future of golf at Gleneagles, with its five tees and contemporary styling. Four courses, three eighteen- and one nine-hole, assure variety as well as scenic splendor; lessons and equipment are available at the pro shop for players of every level.

In addition to offering off-road driving, shooting (target and skeet) and fishing, another superlative attraction is the Equestrian School. Staffed by experienced coaches and well-trained horses, all skill levels are welcomed. From sitting a horse for the first time to trail rides, dressage, side saddle, show-jumping, cross country and carriage driving, there is opportunity for beginners as well as accomplished riders to hone their horsemanship in an ideal environment.

Also in the great European outdoor tradition, Gleneagles offers the ancient sport of falconry, which for centuries has fired the imagination of poets and princes. Under the tutelage of expert falconers, guests can learn the basics of handling and flying Harris hawks. These are great centuries-old birds of prey with a four-foot wingspan, which search out mammals, birds, and reptiles, often hunting in groups. Hawking in the heather and gorse of the Perthshire hills is a sensory thrill: heather-scented air, the tinkling of soft bells, the whoosh of wings swooping toward gloved fists, the taut grasp of talons as the hawk steadies to the hand. It is the stuff of royalty and of legend.

Though the size of accommodations varies, the refined elegance does not. The addition of Baird House, a 59-room annex with deluxe accommodations increases the hotel's appeal as a destination resort. Additionally, 50 new timeshare units have been added. And though its looks are aristocratic, the meticulously maintained Regency hotel is operated in a casual and friendly manner.

Suites are appointed with double-glazed French windows, plush carpeting, antique furnishings, and all the most modern electronic conveniences like CD and DVD players, fax machines, and Internet connections. Good solid wood furniture, crisp sheets, plush towels, and outstanding service are all standard.

Inspiration for the palette comes directly from the Scottish landscape, capped by an ever-changing sky: violet and mauve, autumnal gold and mushroom, deep clear blues.

Other standard equipment includes safes, minibars, and trouser presses. The large baths have claw foot tubs, radiant floor heat, robes, anti-fog mirrors, heated towel racks, and a wide array of toiletries.

Dining at Gleneagles shifts between casual and formal, from the snacks of the Clubhouse bar and grill offering burgers, cold cuts and cheeses, to the classic, extravagant Mediterranean cuisine of the Strathearn restaurant, with its curved dining room opening off the hotel's grand corridor. The Fairlie, named after Gleneagles' master chef, and the only restaurant in Scotland awarded two Michelin stars, has won acclaim for its modernized Scottish menu (the authentic Scottish shortbread is a culinary marvel). Another fine restaurant, in the health center, serves hybrid Italian-California fare.

In keeping with Gleneagles' sporting theme, there is a large lap pool for serious swimmers as well as a warm lagoon surrounded by Egyptian murals and punctuated with a tented Jacuzzi and volcano water-spout. The hotel Spa is a genuine den of self-improvement—spacious treatment rooms decorated with Celtic knots provide detailed beauty treatments like Thai mud therapies, algae wraps, full-body aromatherapy, and a serious, tension-relieving style of body massage. Sauna and steam, plus a complete pro-style fitness center with free weights and machines, are available 24/7.

Far from remote—the cultural and historical attractions of Edinburgh and Glasgow are only an hour away—Gleneagles is an idyllic, accessible hub for all the best in luxury repose and sporting activity that Scotland has to offer.

Mateya Safari Lodge

Fusing visions of primordial wildlife with art depicting Africa's rich history, Mateya beckons visitors seeking outdoor adventure while basking in contemporary luxury.

Here the picturesque and mysterious Dark Continent of legend, birthplace of humanity, still exists. Set in South Africa's Madikwe Game Reserve, the Lodge, which offers sweeping vistas of rolling savannah, just a short distance northwest of Johannesburg, between the Dwarsberg Mountains and Kalahari Desert, is one of the most beautiful and exotic destinations on earth.

Three game rangers are on hand to guide guests on intimate, individualized expeditions (no more than ten at a time). Land Cruisers equipped with radios, coolers, and night sight field glasses venture deep into the bush for up-close viewing of some of the world's most splendid animals, including, of course, the Big Five: elephants, rhinoceroses (both black and white), lions, leopards, and buffalo. Cheetahs, zebras, giraffes, and the now-protected wild dogs, along with numerous species of African bird, may be seen in full regalia and make exciting subjects for camera or camcorder. Sightings of kills are frequent, as are the births of calves during springtime.

The five guest suites and common areas are separated by kopjes, or hills, for maximum privacy. Each suite has sliding glass doors for a constant view of the bush—whether relaxing on the rosewood deck or splashing in the infinity-edge pool, no other quarters are visible; all that can be seen are the endless grasslands and the animals that pass by.

The suites have the feel of 19th-century Africa, the Africa of Stanley and Livingston and Sir Richard Burton—lodges possess gun poles and thatched roofs, with colonial-style mahogany chests, four-poster beds, mahogany armoires, soft, plush sofas and ottomans, and fireplaces everywhere. Baths have free-standing soaking tubs and glass doors, the better to observe the country, and both indoor and outdoor showers.

Suites are also adorned with stunning original African art. There are bronze sculptures and votive figures, oil and water color paintings by noted artists, tribal masks, even wood doors salvaged from a palace in Zanzibar. Sculptor Robert Glen's Near Miss, a lifelike rendition of a lioness lunging at a leaping impala, is one of the signature works at Mateya.

The bar and lounge, open, airy, with a breathtaking view of Hemingway's beloved green hills, and the small but well-stocked library containing a rare collection of African literature dating to 1800, are decorated with

Ardmore pottery and hand-carved wood chairs; in quiet seclusion guests can sip a brandy and relive the continent's uniqueness through the eyes of talented authors. Mateya's health therapist offers the ultimate in massage, along with a full range of body treatments; manicures and pedicures are available in the Wellness Center; and there is a personalized gym with aerobic and weight-training equipment, including a full-size outdoor Jacuzzi.

The cuisine is pure local fare, utilizing homegrown ingredients to delight the palate with a harmony of flavors and textures: fresh produce and choice cuts of meat and fish. Mateya boasts an extensive Hermés china collection, and each evening a different setting is used for dinner. Dining al fresco before the roar of open-air fires, under a canopy of stars, conveys the essence of Africa—the majesty of its eternal land. The Lodge's wine cellar boasts an impressive collection of local as well as rare French wines and champagnes, with over 8,000 bottles of nearly every vintage stocked.

For the sophisticated traveler in search of adventure in a mythic landscape, Mateya Safari Lodge offers an exquisite and luxurious African experience.

Clayoquot Wilderness Resort & Spa

Located in the Clayoquot Sound Reserve on Vancouver Island, British Columbia, this sumptuous resort has grown into a golden triangle of adventure and rusticating luxury, offering visitors a taste of how the well-heeled "roughed it" some hundred years ago.

An enclave of twenty three great white canvas guest suite tents for dining, lounging, and spa treatments, the Wilderness Outpost at Bedwell River is a nature-lover's paradise of scenic splendor. It offers the perfect starting point for an exploration of virgin wilderness with its rich diversity of Canadian wildlife. Guests can participate in animal-migration studies, bear-mapping, bird-watching, even whale-feeding in the nearby Pacific. Designated a Biosphere Reserve by UNESCO, the Bedwell River Valley and rainforest can be traversed on foot, on horseback, or by canoe.

The critically-acclaimed food, Chef Tim May's trademark modern natural cuisine, harmonizes with the rustic setting. Each dish begins with the same three ingredients: fresh, local, and honest. "A Ucluelet dairy," May says, "supplies cheese; 'Oyster Jim' grows the best oysters, and a natural healer living nearby in a floating art studio/organic garden supplies produce in exchange for the occasional long-distance phone call."

Two spa-treatment tents provide deep relaxation and sensory pleasures such as hot tubs, hot stone, Swedish and Thai massage, plus reflexology, aromatherapy, and spa manicures/pedicures. The tents and massage platforms cantilever out over rolling scenes of the Bedwell River estuary and its intertidal exchange of birds, bears, and otters. Gentle, languid pursuits like morning stretch or yoga classes enhance the feeling of oneness with the natural world.

The Clayquot Wilderness Resorts & Spa promises discriminating travelers an ultra-luxurious eco-resort, delightful coastal cuisine, and some of the most strikingly beautiful wilderness frontier left on earth.

Heli-Hiking

————◆————

Heli-hiking takes you to the top of the world.

Explore high-destination altitudes in Calgary, Canada, that can only be accessed by helicopter. The only footprints there are the ones you leave behind.

This expedition gives new meaning to the word "exclusive." Heli-hiking takes guests to the summits of the rarely-visited Columbia Mountains and deposits them there for views of the earth that exceed anything seen from the ground. Smaller mountain ranges spread out beneath you; canyons descend as if reaching straight into the earth's core then disappear under a blanket of cloud. Mountain goats stand only feet away, surprised that you could join them up here in their hard-to-reach terrain.

Certified by the International Federation of Mountain Guide Associations, expert guides are there for edification and assistance. The certificates mean that the guide has met the highest, most stringent standards in rock and alpine climbing proficiency, technical expertise, and environmental consciousness. But guests, not guides, set the pace.

Experienced hiker? Challenge yourself to a rigorous work-out and beat your personal best. Beginner? Take a leisurely walk and let the splendors of nature sink into your soul. But these labels become meaningless by the end of the day—when everyone becomes a bona fide "mountain person." The thrill of being up there is transformative.

The splendor of the surrounding mountains is echoed in the lodges. Each accommodation is the pinnacle of rustic chic. The Adamants, Bobbie Burns, Bugaboo, Caribou and, in particular, Valemount Lodges offer the most hospitable, extravagant services to off-set the ruggedness of their surroundings. There are also amenities such as full-body massages and game rooms for the kids.

The suites are spacious and comfortable, emulating elements of the outdoors. But it's difficult to focus on interior décor when you've seen what's outside your window.

Food actually tastes better at this elevation! It must be something about the air…or the lodges' gourmet chefs—all members of the international Chaîne des Rôtisseurs. Each hotel has a cozy, family-style dining room serving modern variations of hardy, Western fare made from local Canadian ingredients. Or, for a gourmet burger with a side of scenery, eat outside at the Grill by Lunch Lake.

After an adventurous day of heli-hiking, what can be better than relaxing in an outdoor whirlpool, enjoying the snow-capped mountains wrapped in warmth? There's only one possible answer: Heli-skiing the next day!

Heli-hiking takes guests somewhere between heaven and earth, to mountains so remote that some of them have never been named. Very few people other than fellow heli-hikers have even set foot there. After experiencing this elevation, it's hard to ever see the world the same way again.

"*Within a chain of breathtaking islands lies a particular crescent-shaped beach of unsurpassed beauty…*"

Sand Between Your Toes

It takes more than salt water and pink sunsets to earn a place on my recommended list of prestige resorts. It takes virginal islands hidden beneath coco-palms. Over-water bungalows hovering above crystal lagoons. Outdoor massages with ocean views. Reef diving and wind surfing before lunch on linens. These are the traits of true resort luxury.

Las Ventanas al Paraiso

Chic. Sultry. Utterly secluded. Las Ventanas al Paraiso combines the sensuality of Mexico with the sophistication of the Mediterranean; it is not just The Windows to Paradise—it is paradise redefined.

This modern, sexy resort is situated on the coast of Mexico's Baja Peninsula, where an unlimited expanse of tropical desert encounters endless sea. The unexpected juxtaposition of these landscapes is carried over into Las Ventanas' architecture, where the soft curves of adobe walls blend with the white, sleekly stylized aesthetic of the Greek islands. The hospitality of grand Mexican haciendas meets the languid allure of Aegean haute chic.

At Las Ventanas, luxury is synonymous with authenticity and local culture is made palpable through sensuous touches: large, tiled murals; colorful pottery; raised pebble walkways hand-laid by artisans; carved cedar woodwork and handcrafted furniture from Guadalajara. All reflect a proud lineage pulsing throughout the land.

These accents are brought together through the resort's crisp, streamlined Cubist silhouette which stands out boldly against a shimmering blue sea.

Within this contemporary setting, Las Ventanas keeps alive a traditional way of life, from softly blowing conch shells announcing whale sightings to the melodious sounds of a teponaztle, an ancient Mexican percussion instrument that wakes guests from their hammocks and transports them to another time.

The resort's expansive suites are both sumptuous and visually striking. Marble showers, Conchuela limestone floors, weaved chairs and beamed ceilings are brought together in a symphony of space and texture. Oceanfront one-bedroom suites bring the sea virtually outside your door, with enchanting views that sweep across white sand and exotic cacti, palms and jagged mountains.

Rooms are replete with private terrace splash pools, open-air showers and bottles of the finest tequila—a mellow ending to a multitude of perfect evenings.

Amenities epitomize cutting-edge cool and indulgent pleasures. Attendants spray guests with a fine mist of Evian water alongside curvy, drop-edge pools. A swim-up bar serves aged tequila and fresh ceviche. Thatched roofs and chaise lounges provide secluded, languid rest amidst stark, other-worldly desert scenes.

Las Ventanas al Paraiso sits beside the Sea of Cortez, an ideal spot for scuba diving, with

underwater crevices to explore as well as old off-shore shipwrecks.

The hotel provides Mini Coopers for guests to map out their own expeditions, leaving well-traveled roads behind as they blaze up the Pacific coast to nearby La Paz missions or Cabo San Lucas nightclubs.

World-class tennis instructors are always on hand in the resort and seven local championship golf courses (designed by Jack Nicklaus, Robert Trent Jones II and other luminaries) wend their way through canyons to the ocean's edge.

Las Ventanas introduced the world to a new cuisine called Baja-Mediterranean. It is best enjoyed on a table on the beach alongside a bonfire and a soundtrack of soft ocean waves. The hotel's Sea Grill offers a flavorful, changing selection of Mexican tapas and a weekly Guaycura barbecue that updates a culinary tradition of ages past.

The resort also caters to the newest trend in travel—pampering pets that guests bring along. In addition to an extensive pet-friendly room service, the staff will set up small puppy cabanas poolside or in suite dog treadmills so pets can partake in the full luxury treatment.

Las Ventanas al Paraiso is a jet-setting destination, both sensual and visually striking. Infused with the warm lyricism of Mexico and bold interpretations of contemporary culture, Las Ventanas exists beyond the edge of expectation.

Little Dix Bay

Within a chain of breathtaking islands lies a particular crescent-shaped beach of unsurpassed beauty known as Little Dix Bay.

Columbus was one of the first visitors and, upon seeing the island's distinctive, hilly silhouette—resembling a curvy woman lying on the sand—he christened it Virgin Gorda ("Fat Virgin"). And travelers have been enchanted by her ever since.

One such tourist was Laurance Rockefeller, who "rediscovered" Virgin Gorda on a Caribbean sailing trip. Though his family had fortunes, Mr. Rockefeller was a conservationist who preferred the riches found only in nature. Acquiring 500 acres of unspoiled land—which had remained virtually unchanged since seducing Columbus—he established a luxury resort to complement Virgin Gorda's inherent grace.

The remarkable result is the secluded Little Dix Bay resort, accessible by a twenty-minute boat ride past emerald islands set against a backdrop of blue. A hotel staff member meets guests at the airport on Beef Island and accompanies them on their journey as they, too, discover the wonders of this untamed oasis.

The design concept of Little Dix Bay is based on understatement, as buildings blend unobstructively into the surrounding landscape. Some forty organic-looking structures were handcrafted from indigenous materials of locally mined stone, bamboo, banana wood and purpleheart, in keeping with the island's aesthetic charms. A few feature thatched, pagoda-style roofs fashioned after ones Rockefeller had seen in his travels of the South Pacific.

The Pavilion, composed of four such Polynesian pyramids, tilted to let in sun and sea, is the center of island life. It is here where guests are first greeted by a lively Caribbean band—and a bottle of rum and mixers for evening enjoyment. Yet these conical rooftops are unseen from the sea to maintain the island's uninhabited appearance.

Designed to integrate with the environment, the resort accommodations are tucked away among coconut palms, sea grape trees and bougainvillaea. The well-appointed guest rooms, suites and villas curve along the half-mile stretch of beach, with white sand serving as welcome mats. Some Beach Front Cottages are positioned on stilts with garden patios on

the ground level, while two- and three-bed-room Luxury Villas comprise the resort's most private enclave.

The rooms' interiors are in sync with what the whole atmosphere has to offer. Peaked ceilings with exposed beams complement the Caribbean's rustic flavor, while the villa's unusual hexagon-shaped bedrooms both maximize privacy and make the most of panoramic sea views.

Décor exudes a low-key luxury and embraces conservation and a reverence for the environment. Handcrafted teak furniture from the Pacific Rim, seashell accents and light natural fibers lend a casual charm to the sun-soaked interiors. Decorative paddle fans twirl overhead and all rooms supply sun umbrellas and walking sticks—a Rockefeller trademark.

As per Rockefeller's request, there are no TVs in guest rooms—nor clocks, which are of little importance here anyway. Outdoor patios or covered living areas provide optimal views—and the pleasure of soothing trade winds.

Suites also have stone terraces with private pools—though the resort's own swimming pool is a showpiece, built around an outcropping of rocks and inspired by the nearby natural baths.

Understandably, many guests never look beyond the beach—considered among the finest in the world—for amusement. A close-by coral reef protects the shore and ensures calm water year-round. It also provides excellent opportunities for snorkeling, especially down to the Wreck of the Rhone, a Royal Mail Ship that sank in 1867 and remains a hidden treasure of the deep.

Private water taxis transport guests to 13 distinct local destinations, such as tours of ancient copper mines or the Caves on Norman Island. Visitors can also partake in scavenger hunts around Virgin Gorda and neighboring islands, Caribbean Pub Crawls by water, Sunset Cocktail Cruises, torch-lit Robinson Crusoe Beach Parties or Black-Tie Barefoot Soirees—which particularly capture the resort's casual chic.

A day excursion to the Baths at Devil's Bay, three miles from Little Dix, introduces guests to Virgin Gorda's most popular natural attraction. These watery grottoes are surrounded by soaring cathedrals of volcanic rock, as old as time itself.

But the ultimate island refuge is the spa at Little Dix Bay. Nine separate treatment cottages are perched dramatically over the island's northern precipice, offering 25-mile views of Caribbean Sea while indulging in the Spice and Coconut Body Bliss and the Sugar Mill Pineapple Mango Glow—which sound good enough to eat.

Since meals are important events in island life, the Pavilion's open-air restaurant offers a Grand Island Buffet and à la carte dishes featuring Caribbean flavors fused with Continental flair. Intimate torch-lit dinners can be arranged beachside and complimentary afternoon tea, complete with English scones and local Johnny cakes, is served on the Pavilion terrace—an affair enjoyed by Queen Elizabeth II.

Rockefeller was a firm believer in employing local people at Little Dix Bay to proudly serve their land and maintain its integrity. In accordance, Virgin Gordians still graciously attend to guests today, glad to introduce their island paradise to the rest of the world.

Montage Resort & Spa

The well-named Montage is located in the heart of one the world's great art colonies, Laguna Beach, pearl of the Southern California coast.

Situated atop this quaint, picturesque town filled with galleries, craft stores, street artists, and curio shops, Montage is built on sheer bluffs overlooking the pounding, foam-flecked surf. With its sweeping panoramas of the Pacific, striking wood and stone crafts-man-style architecture, and lush landscaping, the theme of Montage is artistry: geographic, architectural, and gastronomic.

Inspired by the Early California Arts and Crafts movement, the resort displays works by noted regional artists, including a porcelain-tiled wall depicting sea life; an ornate bronze sculpture of a California landscape; and an in-laid pate de verre style glass work located at the entrance.

The 262-room hotel stretches across thirty verdant acres and features distinctive turn-of-the-20th-century styling: crown moldings, wainscoting, rich dark woods, period light fixtures, copper gutters, and shingle-type roofing. The craftsman-style stone architecture, complemented by lush shrubbery and winding stone pathways, is reminiscent of a country estate. Gardens showcase a diversity of flowers, trees, and native plants.

In addition to private balconies with spectacular ocean views, each guestroom is lavishly-appointed in every detail. High-tech amenities include DVD players, cordless phones, and 27-inch flat screen televisions.

Beds are layered with feather-top mattresses and goose-down pillows, and feature 400-thread-count linens. The baths, with separate showers, contain veined marble vanities and deep, oversized soaking tubs with marble surrounds wide enough for a bottle and wine glasses; a multitude of candles and bath amenities, including plush robes, underscore the elegance. A 3-to-1 guest-to-staff ratio ensures immediate and exquisite attention, whether for valet parking, 24-hour room service or evening turndown.

Restaurants and lounges offer acclaimed international haute-cuisine as well as solid provincial fare. Studio, the signature restaurant, with its open-air windows and broad Pacific vistas, features original dishes by Chef James Boyce which include pan-seared smoke trout brandade and roasted Greek Orata with balsamic-marinated grilled treviso and asparagus. The Mosaic restaurant offers salads and grilled seafood; the Loft is casual, serving breakfast and lunch prepared country-style; and the resort's centerpiece, the Lobby Lounge, featuring live entertainment, serves cocktails and English teas

as well as a wide choice of domestic and imported wines.

The hotel features three huge pools with individual surrounding cabanas. The white sands of the shore braced by the Laguna cliffs are only a few steps away. The ocean-front SPA Montage and salon feature the ultimate in health services, fitness, and relaxation. Its array of treatments include aromatherapy, algae cellulite massage, botanical baths, clay wraps, reflexology, clay body-sculpting, prenatal massage, and a plethora of therapeutic and sports massages. The spa's spacious fitness center is replete with all the newest computerized resistance and life-cycle equipment—bikes and treadmills—and offers steam room, sauna, lap pool, and cold plunge for post-exercise rejuvenation.

From its stunning architecture and decor to its superb cuisine and world-class service, the Montage offers an unparalleled mix of scenic grandeur, art, and quintessential luxury.

Elounda Beach Hotel & Resort

Rising out of the Aegean Sea of Homer's *The Odyssey*, the 5,000-year-old island of Crete stands as a monument to great civilizations and today boasts one of the most captivating and opulent resorts this side of the gods' Mount Olympus, the Elounda Beach Hotel and Villas.

Located at Aghios Nicolaos on Crete's rugged northeast coast, the 215-room hotel features Royal suites with individual decks leading to the ocean, heated indoor and private outdoor swimming pools in a secluded garden or on the waterfront, and gym rooms with trainer, valet, chef, and pianist. Additionally, the new Imperial Penthouse suite provides an in-house movie theater, and 24-hour dedicated butler. Visited regularly by many international celebrities, the facilities and service at Elounda are more than equal to the rigorous demands and unique needs of a discerning clientele.

The hotel is modern and equipped with the latest electronic devices like fax machines, personal computers and the Internet (even the curtains open electronically). Yet it also features a touch of Greek architecture. Room décor combines Greek-contemporary with a maritime motif befitting an island that has historically made its living from the sea. Interiors unveil thoughtful details in every room, from the handmade furniture to the lavish marble bathrooms to the handsomely trimmed sisal rugs. The teak parquet floors optimally enhance the blue, cream, and white fabrics, spreads, and drapes that accent the guestrooms. Scattered bungalows offer a full range of high-end amenities such as 24-hour room service and whirlpool tubs.

Fun in the Greek sun can take the form of wind surfing, Laser sailboating, deep sea fishing, jet and water-skiing, scuba-diving, or merely paddling about in the saltwater pool. There are nine restaurants and bars from which to choose, including jetty, pool, piano, and harp bars, offering international as well as local Mediterranean cuisine, and a disco. In keeping with Elounda's over-the-top luxury ethos, Maine lobster is flown in fresh from across the Atlantic on request.

Also containing a fully-equipped, state-of-the art fitness center, an aqua gym, a Spa, beauty salon, shopping arcade, and heliport, Elounda Beach Hotel is the epitome of extravagant luxury located on an idyllic, legendary island.

Hotel Bora Bora

A tropical paradise conjuring up images of sailing ships and grass-skirted natives dancing beneath luscious cocopalms, the island of Bora Bora remains one of French Polynesia's most romantic retreats.

Operated by amanresorts, the Hotel Bora Bora, situated 230 kilometers northwest of Tahiti on the island of Bora Bora, is surrounded by one of the world's loveliest, bluest lagoons. Enjoying the best location on the island, the hotel offers the white powdery sands of Matira Beach and excellent snorkeling. Hotel Bora Bora was the first in the archipelago to introduce the enchanting overwater bungalows.

These thatch-roofed, stylish cottages-there are fourteen of them, all air-conditioned-feature two-tiered teak sundecks with steps leading directly into the lagoon and slender piers running to shore. From here, viewing the infinite expanse of the multihued South Pacific is an almost spiritual experience.

Overwater bungalows include a king-size four-poster bed languorously draped with white linen, a ball-and-claw cast iron tub with separate shower, and wicker and rattan love seats and easy chairs. Superior bungalows are at or near the beach and contain sitting areas in addition to the spacious bedrooms. Some offer spectacular views of Mount Otemanu, Bora Bora's tombstone-like mountain.

Faré is the Tahitian word for home. Set in tropical gardens or on the beachfront, the Bora Bora's farés or villas are the hotel's largest accommodations. They contain a living room, bedroom, en suite sitting room, and large sundeck. Perfect for honeymooners, only 12 garden farés have a private swimming pool complete with lounge chairs and dining table.

Activities here are virtually limitless. Water sports, practically invented in this part of the world, include scuba-diving amidst the colorful and exotic marine life, snorkeling, sailing, deep-sea fishing, outrigger canoeing, and barrier reef excursions.

The cuisine at the Bora Bora is typical French Polynesian fare, highlighted by fresh seafood embellished with tomatoes, peppers, cucumbers, and an array of South Sea spices, served along with original island drinks. The Matira Terrace Restaurant and Bar, with its dazzling sunset views, features local musicians and dancers who provide Polynesian cultural entertainment. Lunch can be taken at the Pofai Beach Bar, while afternoon tea is served daily at the Raititi Lounge.

Besides two tennis courts, a half basketball court, a library and a boutique, the Hotel Bora Bora provides in room Marù Spa treatments, the most authentic Polynesian experience in the Pacific. They offer traditional Tahitian or Indonesian massages using pure Tiare Tahiti Monoi. It is an intimate experience in tune with the feeling of serenity that pervades the whole hotel. While enveloping guests in first-class accommodations, the Hotel Bora Bora offers the perfect starting point for a romantic, adventuresome South Seas vacation on an island paradise.

"The Four Seasons Istanbul sits at the crossroads of East and West, where the Orient Express still runs and the moonlight on the Bosporous is irresistible."

City-Scapes

Allow us to direct you to the inter-section of towering skyscraper and pulsing nightlife, the cornerstones of style and culture: the City of Light and the Big Apple; Bond Street and the Bahnhofstrasse; La Scala and The Met. The accent is on style and luxury in the world's great cities.

The Lanesborough

Regal Olde England meets Suave Swinging London, all under one distinguished roof.

Within The Lanesborough's classical façade-the same frame that housed St. George's hospital, drafted by master architecture William Wilkins, who also designed the National Gallery-a marble lobby awes guests with grand columns that rise to high ceilings and stately Regency furniture.

Then one sees it-the glass-roofed Conservatory, strikingly decorated in the style of Brighton Pavilion, with an eclectic mix of chinoiserie, exotic palms, Oriental figurines, vases and lanterns, in an explosion of color and texture that rivals the city's famed street markets.

The Conservatory is known for its proper afternoon teas-voted the best in London by the British Tea Council-served among softly trickling fountains and piano. This decorum gives way to raucous Supper Dances with live jazz on Saturday evenings.

While the Lanesborough's ninety-five suites and guest rooms, each uniquely decorated, are the height of impeccable English taste and individuality, the 1820s furnishings-handsome armoires, in-laid mahogany desks, silk wall coverings, gilded sphinx statues-actually conceal the latest 21st-century technology. Most suites' brocaded curtains open to superb views of Hyde Park's Constitution Arch.

Among the room's formal flourishes of magnificent antiques, oil paintings and fleur-de-lis are personal accents such as bright bowls of fruit and assorted sweets, replenished daily, as if in one's own drawing room.

The Lanesborough's Royal Suite is, at 2,900 square feet of neo-classical splendor, one of the largest in the U.K. In keeping with the site's original occupant-the second Viscount of Lanesborough's 18th-century mansion was built here-the Royal Suite incorporates interior décor befitting a fine private residence: parquet flooring, handmade rugs, chandeliers from casts by Arnold Montrose, marble Regency fireplaces and a hand-painted, cast-iron, roll-top bath.

Both the building's exterior and interior were meticulously restored under the supervision of the Victorian Society and English Heritage, in order to preserve its authentic, august presence.

In addition to the Suite's formal entertaining area, consisting of living room, dining table for ten, and a separate study, there are three bedrooms tastefully done in royal tones of blue and gold or the masculine greens and burgundy of local pubs. As a backdrop, the master bedroom affords views of Constitution Hill.

The English reputation for consummate service is upheld-in fact, elevated-by the Lanesborough's private butlers, who serve guests with aplomb and the utmost discretion. Upon arrival, butlers press a change of clothing for guests and present them with personalized printed business cards and stationery. The hotel also employs a fleet of drivers to take guests around the celebrated sights of London.

Local society visits the Lanesborough for its Library Bar, which evokes the essence of

Britain's legendary private clubs. With rich mahogany paneling and rows of first editions, the Bar provides a more staid sanctuary than the riotously decorated Conservatory.

The Library Bar also houses the renowned Liquid History collection of some of the world's oldest and rarest cognacs, vintages that mark significant historical moments-the inception of the U.S. Library of Congress in 1800 and the start of World War I. Nothing complements cognac quite like one of the Library's rare and high-prized pre-Castro cigars.

In contrast to the Library's timeless mien, the Lanesborough's Spa Studio is a work of fanciful design and wit. The décor makes use of violet lighting, smoked glass and trompe l'oeil furnishings that cheekily reference classical English interiors. The spa offers an extensive assortment of treatments, including such playful packages as Girls' Night In and Ladies Who Lunch.

Ideally located, the Lanesborough is a short stroll from Harrod's and the posh shops of Sloane Street, as well as such venerable institutions as the Victoria and Albert Museum and Buckingham Palace. Despite Britain's enduring love of national monuments and landmark architecture, the true heart of London remains its public parks.

Straddling Hyde Park Corner and illustrious Knightsbridge, the Lanesborough Hotel integrates both the casual and formal aspects of the city, reflecting British tradition with contemporary flair.

The Ritz-Carlton, Central Park

The Ritz-Carlton's rooms? Luxe. Amenities? The latest. Atmosphere? Lots. Location? New York City, baby—there's nothing else like it!

On the edge of Central Park, mid-town Manhattan, center of the universe, stands The Ritz-Carlton New York, Central Park, an enduring 33-story icon of sophistication and cosmopolitan chic.

The Ritz's guest rooms impart a relaxed, residential feel—though at 850 square feet, The Deluxe Park View Suite puts most residents' studio apartments to shame. These posh accommodations feature one bedroom—with feather bed—and two full baths, plus a large walk-in closet well-suited for world travelers. An in-room telescope gives close-up views of Central Park, the metropolis' most celebrated public space.

While the rooms' swanky interiors recall the charm of Old New York, with brocaded drapes and ornamental carpets, they also come equipped with the highest standards of communication, high-speed Internet and multi-line cordless phones with voicemail and data capabilities. A Technology Butler is on call to help keep guests' laptops and faxes up and running—this is, after all, a city of constant motion.

The hotel's premiere room is the Ritz-Carlton Suite, resembling an uptown penthouse. This 21st-floor, 1,908-square-foot suite has two bedrooms, a living room with a well-stocked library of books on art, architecture and the city's diverse history, a dining room that seats eight and 2½ baths—with 12-inch flat screen TVs in the master bathroom. The entertainment system includes an exceptional selection of CDs. So throw open the window, crank up Sinatra and get ready to go out on the town.

In New York, exclusivity is key. So The Ritz-Carlton's Club Level, an upscale, second-floor retreat available only to guests, is the place to kick back in style, surrounded by

fresh flowers, soft music and panoramic views of Central Park and skyscrapers. The Club supplies international newspapers, periodicals and wireless laptops, as well as backgammon, chess and checkers boards to brush up on your game before facing the formidable players in Washington Square Park.

The top-shelf amenities at The Ritz-Carlton are as eclectic as the city itself: An extensive caviar menu at Atelier, the modern French restaurant. A Bath Butler who makes sure a hot soak awaits. An overnight shoeshine service to get you ready to hit the city streets. An in-house Gemologist. And La Prairie spa, with Manhattan Minutes quick massages and pedicures for those on the run.

While The Ritz-Carlton is a destination in itself, everything you could ever want is right outside its doors. Within walking distance is Fifth Ave, the city's predominant shopping district. Christian Dior, Louis Vuitton and Bergdorf Goodman all reside in this neighborhood, next to cultural luminaries like The Metropolitan Museum of Art, Carnegie Hall and Lincoln Center. But, despite the city's world-class restaurants, make sure to grab a pretzel from the corner street vendor.

That's what New York is all about—a mix of urban hip and Upper West Side suave. And, at one of the most prestigious addresses in the world, The Ritz-Carlton stands in the heart of it all.

The Ritz-Carlton, Central Park

Peninsula Beverly Hills

Set in the most prestigious area of Los Angeles and a stone's throw from the glamour of Hollywood's Rodeo Drive, the four-story Peninsula Beverly Hills has the look and feel of a rarefied country estate rather than a hotel in a western metropolis.

Used to serving the avant-garde—actors, rock stars, writers, and businessmen—privacy and extraordinary service are bywords with staff. For instance, the hotel's Rolls Royce is available to chauffeur guests about at no charge during business hours within Beverly Hills. Here, plush accommodations nestled in tropical gardens swaddle guests in luxurious quietude, while celebrated restaurants offer the perfect atmosphere for dining in high style.

The residential-type guest quarters are replete with antiques and fine art. The gorgeous 1,150 square-foot California Suite has polished hardwood floors that lend a distinct California feel to this one bedroom beauty. The California also features a separate living area, a dining table for six, and a separate guest powder room.

Villas, magnificent bungalow-style hideaways, are located amidst the gardens and offer king size beds, fireplaces, patios on ground level, and double sinks in the bathroom. They also feature French doors, marble-trimmed fireplaces and private outdoor Jacuzzis. Rooms contain a full gamut of electronic amenities; as a courtesy to international guests, radios are equipped to receive short-wave transmissions.

The Peninsula is located on Santa Monica Boulevard and Wilshire, making it the perfect vantage point for touring Los Angeles. Whether strolling past Rodeo Drive's exquisite stores, visiting Graumann's Theater and the Sunset Grill, cruising Mulholland Drive beside the mansions of film icons like Charlie Chaplin and Errol Flynn, or surfing the breakers at Malibu, there is an abundance of activities and sights within the hotel's proximity.

Dining choices range from casual al fresco at the Roof Garden restaurant to the world-class The Belvedere, featuring Executive Chef Sean Hardy. Formerly Lead Chef Instructor at the Culinary Institute, he was part of the team that helped the Belvedere garner the coveted Mobil Four-Star Award in 2005 and maintain the AAA Five Diamond Award for ten years.

Featuring a creative and distinctive modern American cuisine, The Belvedere serves a superb breakfast, lunch and dinner. Menu highlights include Peeky Toe Crab Cakes with

poached eggs and hollandaise for breakfast; Potato Crusted California Sturgeon with an orange reduction and fresh dill for lunch; and for dinner Truffle Roasted Chateaubriand of Veal with forest mushrooms.

As might be expected from this posh hotel in the heart of Beverly Hills, the Peninsula's Spa facilities and treatments do justice to the Sun King's Versailles palace. Poolside massage is available for couples in heated cabanas that surround the sixty-foot pool. While they relax on beds of rose petals and listen to soft jazz, therapists combine jasmine, sandalwood and lavender emollients with Swedish pressure-point massage to promote maximum relaxation and balance energy; every cutting edge treatment and technique known to the finest therapists is available at the Peninsula.

In keeping with the California fitness lifestyle, exercise equipment is extensive and top notch. The fitness center provides a grand view of the city and contains the very latest technology, including Cybex resistance machines and Precor Treadmill Trotters fitted with individual flat screen TVs and disposable headphones. There are Tectrix Stair Climbers and Bikes, hand weights, adjustable benches, and private trainers constantly available to assist in workouts.

In addition to steam, sauna, and cold plunge rooms, the Spa offers fitness beverages and foods like cholesterol-free eggs with tomato and basil, grilled Pacific swordfish with pineapple, basil and key lime vinaigrette, and a host of fruit smoothies, herbal teas, and specially imported elixir tonics.

Even the most sophisticated globe-trotters will appreciate the style and luxury of this magnificent and exclusive hotel.

Peninsula Beverly Hills

103

The Ritz London

Though French by design, The Ritz London is a quintessentially English establishment-the epitome of a grand hotel where service is serious business and afternoon tea is an institution in itself.

The Ritz is an iconic London landmark opened in 1906 by César Ritz-introducing the world to a new word and to a new level of luxury and opulence never before experienced in a hotel. That standard of excellence has been upheld and refined in the last 100 years, earning The Ritz the distinction of being the first hotel ever awarded the Royal Warrant from Prince Charles.

The seven-story Ritz is centrally situated in London's West End on the edge of Green Park, just 500 yards from Buckingham Palace. This elite location extends into The Ritz's hallowed interior where service is paramount and exceedingly proper. Staff, outfitted in traditional tailcoats, outnumbers guests two to one and the formal dress code in the hotel's public areas-jackets for men; no jeans-keeps guests looking at home in their posh environment.

The rooms have preserved a patina of warmth and welcoming from the original turn-of-the-century interior. Conjuring images of a French château, accommodations have a Belle Epoque appeal with fabrics restored to the original Louis XVI style and 24-carat gold-leaf antique furnishings.

The 133 guest rooms are all lushly decorated in The Ritz's signature color schemes of soft blues, pinks, peaches and yellows-a coherent refrain that resonates throughout the building's décor. Edwardian leather-topped desks, silk upholstered headboards and suites with marble fireplaces designate The Ritz as the second home to the world's most famous and fashionable.

While all quarters are quiet and showcase the beauty of the surrounding city, with views of residential Westminster or Arlington, spacious corner suites overlook Green Park gardens. For the best views, the Green Park Suites, with high ceilings, and Piccadilly Suites, with two baths and interconnecting bedroom options, offer grandeur and luxury in a regal ambience.

The Ritz Suites shimmer with white, à la francaise furniture cloaked in luscious brocades with gold tones that echo the taps in the baths. These sizable rooms feature well-stocked minibars, vanities full of luxurious toiletries and fireplaces that glimmer through London fog.

The Ritz's Palm Court is a testament to consummate taste, impeccable style and enduring tradition. London society takes tea amidst its bursting bouquets, grand crystal chandeliers, gold statues and marble fountains-making it essential to reserve six weeks in advance.

The Ritz Restaurant provides the city's most sought-after dining experience. Its modern and classic European selections are served in gilded splendor to well-dressed guests (jacket and tie are required even for lunch); a

table set discreetly in the corner is always reserved for the Queen. The Restaurant hosts orchestra dances on weekend evenings, which are noted social events.

The Rivoli Bar is a time-honored shrine to socializing. With bold design details from the birth of Art Deco, including Lalique glass panels, carved camphor wood, gold keystone nuggets and faux leopard skin furniture, the Rivoli sets the standard for swank entertaining. Cocktails and canapés are served among etched glass windows that look out onto Piccadilly.

The Ritz Club, the hotel's lower level casino, offers a spectrum of gaming in Edwardian grandeur. Winnings can be well-spent on nearby Bond Street, the epicenter of designer shopping, on a custom-tailored suit from Saville Row or in neighboring Fortnum and Mason, perhaps the most "English" of London's department stores with its genteel atmosphere and Old World wares.

From its privileged location to its posh interiors, The Ritz London is a classic-as beloved as Big Ben and as British as Buckingham Palace.

Le Meurice

Glimmering with a Gallic splendor that could only be produced in the City of Light, Paris' Hotel Meurice is the architectural equivalent of a majestic Jacques-Louis David hanging in the nearby Louvre.

The hotel faces the Jardin des Tuileries, the original, elaborately formal garden of the Bourbon kings which remains today as a public park. The property has greatly benefited from being acquired by the Sultan of Brunei, whose massive renovations have made the Meurice first among such French palaces as the Crillon, the Ritz, and the George V.

In the heart of the city—three blocks from the Place de la Concorde and only a few steps from the boutiques and jewelry stores on the legendary Rue de la Paix—the hotel sits in one of the most historic spots in all Europe, where many of the principal events of the French Revolution, Napoleonic period, Bourbon Restoration, and Paris Commune took place.

Its sit-down reception and long conciergerie counter sparkle under crystal chandeliers in a circular entrance area with eight-foot white and gold china lamps. Bustling attendants wear the old-fashioned bellmen's caps.

The Meurice's suites are among the most lavish in France. Boasting a total of 160 soundproof, 19th-century-styled rooms, some suites, like the top-floor Belle Etoile, offer panoramic 360 degree views of Paris, framed by the Tuileries, Arch de Triumphe, Notre Dame, and the Eiffel Tower glittering in the evening like a pearl spike. The 3,000-square-foot terrace has a stone floor, hand crafted wood furniture, and thick, luxuriant green foliage.

Rooms are individually decorated with fine art, plush carpeting, marble statuary, and damasked and brocaded fabrics. Several have painted ceilings of puffy clouds and blue skies, along with canopied beds. Bathrooms are spacious and brightly-lit, some with Jacuzzis; all have hand-carved moldings and mosaic floors. The thick, soft beds are trimmed in period fabrics and the finest linens, giving each a look of regal elegance. In fact, Queen Victoria once spent several nights here, as did the Russian composer Peter Tchaikovsky.

The lavish, ornate Restaurant Le Meurice offers exquisite French haute cuisine like blue lobster in chateau chalon wine sauce and chicken stuffed with foie gras. Le Jardin d'Hiver, with an Art Nouveau-style glass roof which allows light to bathe the palms and 19th-century-style furniture, was recently restored in order to summon sun and moonlight in a grand way. It offers a lighter, less formal menu and a diverse selection of teas, served daily along with French pâtisseries, traditional scones and finger sandwiches.

Then there is an assortment of other-worldly French pastries from renowned pastry chef Camille Lesecq, including his signature masterpiece "le Millefeuille comme vous l'aimez." This divine concoction blends classic chocolate pastry with a choice of chocolate, coffee, or vanilla bourbon cream filling, and is topped with either grilled pistachio or pine nuts. The chef's simple motto is, "To please oneself and others."

The Bar Fontainebleau offers customers the ultimate in personal taste, with over 50 whiskies and malts available. Patrons may even order Dom Pérignon by the glass, a rarity and a luxury even by Parisian standards.

The Espace Bien-Etre, the hotel spa, features treatments, products and specially trained masseuses from Les Sources de Caudalie, the world's first "vinothérapie" spa. The Pulp Friction full-body massage uses fresh grapes for revitalizing skin, while the Crushed Cabernet Scrub employs a blend of grape seeds and essential oils. A newly-added fitness center features a jet pool, sauna and steam room, and serious, state-of-the art exercise equipment.

The Meurice's magnificent décor has provided the setting for several films, while its salons have hosted many of high society's celebrations. Parisian houses of haute couture including Chanel and Guy Laroche have staged many a reception and fashion show in Le Meurice's fabled salons. Its tradition of outstanding beauty, attention to detail, and unsurpassed service sustains its popularity and continued prestige.

Baur Au Lac

Owned and operated by the same family since 1844, Zurich's Hotel Baur Au Lac, one of the world's grandest and Switzerland's most celebrated landmark, continues a tradition of refined ultra-luxury that has been recognized by much of Europe's royalty over many decades.

Austria's Empress Elisabeth once spent an entire summer here, along with two princes and an entourage of 60; the last Russian Czarina, Alexandra, wife of Nicholas II, stayed at the Baur Au Lac, as did German Emperor Kaiser Wilhelm. Countless stories could be told, were it not for the hotel's discretion which became part of its reputation and lore. One story that can be told is how Baroness Bertha von Suttner convinced Swedish industrialist Alfred Nobel of the need for an international peace prize.

Situated in its own private park on the shore of beautiful Lake Zurich, the hotel sustains the atmosphere of a private family home meticulously maintained down to the tiniest details. The owners constantly prim and preen the place to achieve near perfection in style and service.

A four-story sparkling white classical structure surrounded by verdant gardens and perfectly trimmed ginkgo trees, the Baur Au Lac was at first more of a large villa and served as a deluxe residence for famous guests traveling incognito. Through constant attention, enlargement and improvements, Johannes Baur, its founder, had managed within ten years to create a hotel worthy of kings. The newspaper *Leipziger Illustrierte Zeitung* in 1854 had this to say about the burgeoning resort, already frequented by numerous notables and aristocrats:

> "Art must vie with nature, which displays, even lavishes, all of its charms here. The exterior of the hotel promises a great deal. But when one goes inside and walks through the luxurious salons and bedrooms, all of one's expectations are exceeded."

The same is true today, only more so.

Each suite has been individually designed so that no two are exactly alike. Some may have an Empire piece, a style from one of the Louis periods, or even modern furnishings. While the décor varies from Louis XV to Chippendale and Regency, all have one common characteristic: tasteful opulence.

In rooms where the great composers Richard Wagner and Franz Liszt once entertained at the piano, guests today are treated to Jugendstil glass, tapestries, marble floors and Oriental carpets. Each has deep-pile carpeting, starched linens, and large traditional oak and mahogany built-in closets with drawers (some with sliding luggage racks).

Despite the capacious public areas, the well-chosen, thoroughly professional staff acts as if the hotel were a residence. This discreet familial atmosphere includes the general manager, whose father ran the hotel before him. To maintain exclusivity, groups are never booked, and casual tourists wandering in are discouraged.

Dining at the Baur Au Lac is an outright indulgence. The flagship Restaurant Francais serves some of the most innovative haute cuisine in Europe, while Le Pavillon, more informal, features Mediterranean dishes. In summer guests dine here al fresco on large terraces overlooking the gardens and lake. There is also the Rive Gauche, a brasserie with an East-meets-West menu, designed for a younger crowd, and its adjacent Rive Gauche Bar serving 100 single-malt whiskeys. The long polished wood bar is softly illuminated with art deco lamps imported from New York. The Baur Au Lac's Diagonal Nightclub, on Lake Zurich, is one of the hottest dance clubs in the city.

Activities here, in addition to absorbing the breathtaking Alpine views, include horseback riding, scuba-diving, and waterskiing on Lake Zurich. The fifth-floor fitness club overlooks the lake and offers jogs, sight-seeing walks, and shopping expeditions through the old town of Zurich, in addition to housing the finest fitness equipment: Cybex machines compliment free weights and a large stretching, calisthenics, and aerobic exercise zone. Swimming, massage, and personal training are available 24 hours.

The Hotel Baur Au Lac caters to a cosmopolitan elite and offers unmatched grandeur, style, and service in an idyllic Swiss setting.

Bulgari Hotel Milano

In its first foray into luxury hotels, Bulgari Italian jewelers offer a tribute to the birthplace of high fashion.

The Bulgari Hotel is situated in Milan's most stylish area. Next to the renowned shopping rectangle of Via Spiga and Montenapoleone, the Bulgari resides as an unexpected oasis of stylized tranquility in the center of a burgeoning city.

This sixty-room boutique property was recently built. Its guest rooms and suites are a blend of contemporary design and high technology.

The hotel's interior is a modernist's dream—all clean lines, smooth surfaces and geometric form. Precious materials of black Zimbabwe marble, bronze detailing and Brera stone invoke a design concept of upscale aesthetics and restrained opulence.

Rooms exude a richness of atmosphere through uncluttered space and creamy color schemes that complement bleached oak flooring. A chiascuro play of dark and light is evident in the contrast of black sculptural furnishing and neutral shades of fabric—creating an effect both strikingly bold and serene.

For cutting-edge entertainment, en suite systems feature Tivoli CD players with exquisite sound and large-screen plasma TVs hung like canvasses. Each room also includes a cavernous walk-in closet to accommodate even the most extensive wardrobe—including room for items picked up in town from the season's new collections.

Floor-to-ceiling windows open to scenic views of Milan's historic Brera district and the orange tiled rooftops that typify Italian architecture. Sunlight streaming in through the terrace can be blocked by full-length blackout drapes to ensure seclusion and uninterrupted sleep 'til noon—when espresso is certainly in order.

The Bulgari Suite, on the top floor, represents the height of style with assured, contemporary touches throughout its four rooms: a wall-length slab of Brera stone with cut-out fireplace; a tub carved from a single block of Turkish Bihara stone; a sink of soft Navona travertine.

Surrounding the hotel is 40,000 square feet of set-design gardens. First cultivated 700 years ago, they are an integral part of the hotel's balance between architectural design and organic elements.

A stunning blend of black lilies of the valley, Bordeaux-red hydrangeas and slate stones,

these grounds evoke the essence of historic villa gardens that made up the local landscape. An outdoor garden bar is set in the shade during summer months.

The spa at Bulgari is an urban shelter, its contemporary atmosphere contrasting ancient practices of well-being. A long pool tiled with shining gold and emerald mosaic leads to a glass-enclosed Hamam, a private sanctuary in which to meditate.

The spa also offers in-house image consulting and makeovers by Monica Coppola, one of the country's most sought-after beauty artists.

Bulgari's lounge and restaurant are the epitome of streamlined sophistication. Changing works of contemporary art and silver Bulgari flatware enhance food already bursting with strong flavor and brilliant colors. Hotel chefs use spices from the gardens and local wine is brought in from regions like Sardinia and Sicily.

Near La Scala Opera Theatre and Il Duomo, the Bulgari is a modern addition to the cityscape. Its neighbors are the Botanical Gardens and the Brera district, known for narrow alleyways and nightlife. Guests can rent a Ferrari, Lamborghini or Maserati to see the town in true Italian fashion. And, speaking of fashion, the hotel provides a personal shopper to search for designer pieces that haven't yet arrived stateside.

Exuding the avant-garde design for which both the Bulgari brand and Milan are well-known, the Bulgari Hotel stands as a chic symbol in the heart of haute couture.

Bulgari Hotel Milano

Four Seasons Istanbul

A luxurious and picturesque hotel brimming with history and romance, the Four Seasons Istanbul sits at the crossroads of East and West, where the fabled Orient Express still runs and the moonlight on the Bosporus is irresistible.

Created in 1995 on the site of historic neoclassic Sultanahmet Prison, the city block gave way easily to its new purpose. The hotel's design combines Ottoman Empire-elements with current Western building technology, producing a modern but distinctive Turkish architecture.

The hotel lies in the old town of Istanbul near the mosque of the Sultan Ahmet or Blue Mosque, built by Mehmet Aga, greatest architect of the Ottoman Empire. The prison was named after the 17th-century Ottoman ruler.

The Four Seasons preserved most of the Sultanahmet's original structure, keeping much of the ochre-tinted stone, brickwork, ironwork, marble pillars, decorative tiles, vaulted ceilings and dome-shaped arches and oval porticoes. The interior decoration echoes the late imperial palaces (the Ottoman Empire lasted some 700 years and disintegrated in 1918). It contains myriad mosaic inlays and friezes which, combining with European-style brocaded furniture and glass chandeliers, generate a distinctive Turkish effect. Outside, the courtyards, garden, and paths are reminiscent of Roman Empire-era Byzantium; a high wall skirts the grounds. Shiny mosques and towering minarets punctuate the sprawling city; vibrato-voiced criers can be heard throughout the day calling the Muslim faithful to prayer.

Guestrooms—sixty-five of them—offer king or twin beds and an entertainment armoire with VCP and Bose CD/radios, flat screen TVs and a refrigerated bar; some have fireplaces. Even by Four Seasons standards, the marble bathrooms are remarkably ample and luxurious, with their sumptuous bathtub, separate walk-in shower, and private WC.

All suites are replete with Ottoman art and artifacts. Wood accents are dark and polished, and there are brass fittings everywhere. Impressionistic oil paintings by local artists, craft items and, of course, richly woven Turkish and Armenian carpets abound.

Innovative cuisine incorporating fresh local ingredients is the mainstay of the Four Seasons restaurants. The Seasons offers fine dining, while the Winter Garden serves more casual fare. Menus feature distinctive international and local dishes such as artichoke confit with organic petite vegetables, thyme ricotta cheese and pan-seared shrimp scampi, or garlic-marinated loin of lamb rolls with spinach-stuffed eggplant.

For health and fitness, the hotel Spa offers an assortment of therapeutic massage treatments, including a Balinese technique that utilizes skin-rolling kneads. Aromatherapy, Deep Sport and Citrus Oil massage are also available. The fitness center provides all the newest body sculpting and resistance-training gear, including machines and free weights, as well as computerized cardiovascular equipment.

In a place where the European and Asian continents intersect and great religions merge, activities in Istanbul naturally center round the magnificent sights: the sublime architecture of venerated mosques and churches, the ancient cobbled streets, the Grand Bazaar, the museums, the Tokapi Palace, Roman ruins, and a thousand little shops and stalls selling everything from shish kebob sandwiches to religious icons to Hollywood t- shirts.

Combining Old World charm with contemporary luxury, the Four Seasons Istanbul is the perfect vantage point from which to enjoy the blending of cultures in a beautiful and historic city.

Four Seasons Istanbul

"Alive with the light of the sun or…evening lights…Palmasola villas are an invitation to paradise…"

Villa Life

Make some of the most magnificent places on earth your second home. In luxury travel, nothing is as inviting as villa life, with residences that are architectural statements…all-inclusive service that anticipates every need or want…settings that are unparalleled—and unexpected. Do what you want, when you want—the villa is yours exclusively; the world is yours to explore.

Mustique Island

The simplicity of Mustique Island puts attention on the real pleasures in life—nature's bounty, ocean air and the warmth of sun and friendly smiles.

Once an island of abandoned sugar plantations in the Caribbean, Mustique was later purchased by an English lord for a family estate. Then, a wedding gift, ten acres of this tropical land were given to Princess Margaret, who built a magnificent residence there—appropriately called "Les Jolies Eaux"—immediately elevating the island's status.

Decades later, Mustique was acquired by shareholders from some 20 countries—making it a true global village composed of eclectic influences and flavors. This community is dedicated to maintaining and enhancing the island for generations to come.

Mustique boasts only one hotel—a spectacular one of singular beauty. The Cotton House is a refurbished 18th-century cotton warehouse and sugar mill located directly on the beach, caressed by the Caribbean Sea to the west and the Atlantic Ocean to the east.

This well-situated structure retains some of its original features, restored to their former glory by famed British theatrical designer Oliver Messel, who set the stage for romance. The Cotton House has just 20 rooms and suites, making it one of the best-kept secrets in the Caribbean—and ranking it as one of the Leading Small Hotels in the World.

The nearby Firefly Guest House is an enchanted enclave. Recessed into a hillside, this three-story structure has a front entrance nearly hidden by lush vegetation. With its stone inlaid walls and sunken sun lounges, the villa is an organic extension of the island itself—all the way to the tropical garden setting of its two-tiered swimming pool...with waterfall!

The island itself is a reserve of pure, pristine nature, like the bluish-green beauty of its Britannica Bay. Remotely located at the northern tip of the Grenadines, Mustique is covered with mangrove forests—home to a profusion of tropical wildlife and haven for rare species hardly seen off this island. On charted nature trails, or when resting in hardwood-framed hammocks that dot the resort, guests can glimpse blue herons, smooth-billed anis, tortoises and iguanas. A serene lily pad pond boasts fuschia flowers and families of frogs.

All of this is protected by the island's owners, who are dedicated to preserving the environment—and the privacy of its inhabitants. Under a controlled development plan, there are eighty-nine exclusive villas scattered throughout the island, each with its own unique architectural style. A majority of these exceptional properties is available for weekly rental.

Mustique's main town is a charming little village of sorbet-colored buildings with intricate latticework and airy demeanors. Guests can rent Jeeps, motorcycles or mountain bikes to explore inland and get to know the locals at the Sweetie Pie Bakery or the food store and fish market. Everywhere on the small island of Mustique, the eye uncovers simple, exquisite scenes of enormous beauty.

Palmasola

A premiere beach. Imaginative architecture. Impeccable service. Everything one would expect from villa life—taken to the extreme. On the coast of Mexico, there is only one word for this paradise: Palmasola.

Located in Punta Mita, the 22,000-square-foot Palmasola resort is secluded in a grove of palm trees on a breathtaking white beach. This exclusive, self-contained setting houses eight separate thatched-roofed structures, each an arresting design unto itself and, together, a cohesive luxury village.

While the pool deck is the heart of the complex, it is surrounded by shared areas such as a poolside dining and kitchen palapa, a cozy pool pavilion with beachside firepit, a gym and massage room, caretakers' quarters and an open-air media and family center where guests can watch films or play foosball. The palapas' thatched rooftops seem remote, peeking through thick palm trees, but stand only steps away from the ocean shore.

Accommodations are divided among the spacious two-floor Guest Residence, containing four bedrooms, four baths, two shared living rooms and two private terraces, and the palatial Master Residence, the entire upper level of which is devoted to the master bedroom, bath, dressing room and two private terraces—one with daybeds and the other with heated Jacuzzi.

The residences resemble grand haciendas to harmonize with Mexican history, and each room in these villas is designed around a unique theme. El Mar features solid boat hull bed frames, blue accents and mounted oars to replicate the ocean indoors. El Sol, the master

bedroom, shimmers in iridescent décor, brightly-painted walls and a palm tree four-post bed. The rooms must be seen to be believed—and even then they are unbelievable!

Palmasola's full-service staff is always on call to anticipate every need—from a breakfast bursting with local flavors to a perfect poolside margarita or a beautifully made bed that awaits in the evening—leaving guests to relax in unspoiled comfort. Meals may be served anywhere within the resort—most memorably on the residences' rooftop terraces.

A Cadillac Esplanade SUV with driver is supplied for local trips, which can include a treetop canopy adventure, visits to remote mountain Indian villages or the nearby, renowned Four Seasons Spa. Palmasola itself offers plentiful activities such as a Jack Nicklaus golf course, beach volleyball and equipment for world-class surfing, windsurfing, scuba diving and swimming with dolphins.

Whether alive with the light of the sun or bathed in the warm glow of evening lights, the Palmasola villas are an invitation to paradise—out-of-this-world yet entirely within reach.

Temenos Villas

Slip into a Mykonos-inspired dream—in the middle of the Caribbean.

The three Temenos Villas on Anguilla are modern, rationalist designs of spare purity—all startling white against aqua blue ocean. Villa Sand, Villa Sea and Villa Sky have sleek, clean lines and perfect proportions that make these structures stylized ideals of architecture and suggest an atmosphere of Mediterranean sophistication.

"Temenos" is Greek for "sanctuary"—a theme expressed in the villas' soothing interiors. Villas Sea, Sky and Sand have soft color schemes that reflect their names and subtly convey island surroundings indoors.

Richly textured elements such as marble, granite, wrought iron, woven rugs and mosaic tiles are manifestations of the natural environment, which offset the state-of-the-art kitchen and entertainment equipment.

Island life is all about unconstrained freedom—which the villas recreate in their spacious settings. Soaring cathedral ceilings echo endless sky; light streams in from louvered doors; infinity pools overlook an even more infinite sea.

Enormous indoor marble bathrooms are mirrored in the marble outdoor showers—complete with remote control scrim. Cut-out enclaves in the architecture serve as meditation spaces, resonating with the seclusion of this island oasis.

Anguilla is a small, eel-shaped island with beaches the color and purity of fine stationery. While the resort offers water activities, from scuba diving and snorkeling to yacht and fishing excursions, guests can also explore the pristine shore with surfside horseback riding, yoga classes on the sand or day-long picnics privately catered on the beach.

The cuisine takes its cue from local flavors. Meals are personally planned with Temenos' executive chef and are served in suite, at the outdoor dining pavilion or at water's edge. Guests can also visit the local Koal Keel Restaurant for seaside dining in a restored 18th-century plantation house, where unfussy, faultless fare is served with a side of traditional Anguillan rice 'n peas—a true taste of the island.

Personal butlers pre-stock each villa with guests' favorite foods and a full wet bar, in addition to any requested items, bringing a touch of home to a far-off region.

Any good jeweler knows that the setting is as important as the stone. The Temenos Villas are Greek-inspired gems set into a platinum blue Caribbean Sea.

Exclusive Resorts, Luxury Residence Club

Reversing the maxim that perfection is a journey and not a destination, Exclusive Resorts, a luxury residence club offering access to the most luxurious vacation spots on earth, proves once and for all that perfection is a destination.

With over thirty worldwide locations and hundreds of residences currently in Exclusive Resorts' portfolio, from deluxe apartments in Paris and London to opulent villas in Tuscany to oceanfront homes in the Caribbean, this destination club is a leader in its category. Posh new residences are being built each month, all spacious and combining the amenities of a private home and a luxury resort.

Not to be confused with time shares or 'fractional ownership'-that new buzzword for an old concept-the Exclusive Resorts luxury residence club is a worry-free alternative to purchasing a vacation home. Members gain regular access to various fancy properties in differing climes and locales without the hassle of having to maintain properties hundreds,

even thousands, of miles away. The club enables members to choose from among three different memberships: an Elite, an Executive, and Affiliate. The cost of dues is dependent upon the amount of usage.

When browsing through the Exclusive Resorts portfolio, members learn that the residences highlighted on the page are not necessarily where they will stay. Members and their families will notice that they will be well-attended by a personal Residence Concierge.

Transportation en route as well as during the stay, along with grocery shopping, is conveniently handled by the Concierge, as is coordination of daily maid service. In addition to offering expert advice on sightseeing and activities, the Concierge will also set up golfing tee times, schedule spa treatments and make dinner and theater reservations.

Exclusive Resorts residences in Los Cabos, Mexico, lie within the community of Punta Ballena. The villas are one-story free-standing structures containing three or four bedrooms.

Each has a stunning ocean view and complete resort amenities.

The Villas Las Conchas, with four-bedroom residences, cover 3,500 square feet and offer two spacious ocean view master bedrooms. There are separate guest casitas, indoor and outdoor showers, and swimming pool with personalized spa and waterfall. The very highest quality materials are used in the architecture: natural stone floors, marble vanities and granite countertops.

Residents of the Esperanza Villas have access to the Infinity pool and the Esperanza Spa, considered Mexico's finest, as well as gourmet restaurants including The Mercado, El Bar, and The Restaurant. Personalized breakfast and lunch preparation is available, as is daily maid service.

Telluride, Colorado, is one of the most beautiful spots on earth. The mountains rise high and majestic, offering one of the most fabulous skiing experiences anywhere. Resiences are a short walk from gonadola in what is called Mountain Village. The residence here comprises a whopping 3,000 square feet, with four and a half baths, a private spa set on a deck, and state-of-the-art audio/visual equipment.

World class winter sports like downhill skiing, cross-country skiing, snowboarding, mountain climbing and whitewater rafting are available here.

Exclusive Resorts maintains the largest luxury residence club portfolio with top destinations all across the globe. As a result, a member's greatest challenge is deciding where to vacation next.

Villa la Vigie

Always modern. Stylishly sexy. Villa la Vigie is the essence of Monte Carlo.

With an unparalleled vantage point overlooking the lights of Monte Carlo and the glittering French Riviera, Villa la Vigie is an astounding three-story structure built in the style of a grand mansion. The Villa has six bedroom suites, all bedecked in a medley of Art Deco-inspired chocolate browns and blond wood designed by former owner Karl Lagerfeld, whose name was synonymous for years with Chanel couture. A ground-floor kitchen with the latest appliances, dining and living rooms, a library, private scalloped balconies, outdoor Jacuzzi and game area make for exceptional entertaining.

A caretaker is on site year-round, to assure the reception and comfort of the tenant, and a personal driver, with a Mercedes S-class car, can be requested. Food and beverages are catered by the nearby Monte Carlo Beach Hotel and the Société des Bains de Mer will help arrange banquets and soirees in the Villa's ultra-chic setting, such as the one hosted by Princess Caroline of Monaco for her daughter's eighteenth birthday.

Villa la Vigie crowns a city of exceptional energy and international reputation. Monte Carlo, Europe's virtual private club of cosmopolitan glamour and epicurean nightlife. Home to royalty and celebrated society, the principality also boasts a myriad of bars, restaurants and discotheques, including the beachfront Sea Lounge just downhill from Villa la Vigie.

Monte Carlo retains the year-round atmosphere of a permanent holiday. It is a renowned cultural center, esteemed for its Princess Grace Ballet Academy and the baroque beauty of its Opera House, that also holds such high-adrenaline activities as Formula One Grand Prix racing, the Monte Carlo Open, a prelude to men's French Open tennis, and sequined musical extravaganzas at La Cabaret.

But the city is perhaps best-known for its high-stakes casino gaming. Roulette is played in the ornate Sallee Europe and fortunes ride on each hand in the Salon Privés, roped off to all but the highest rollers. The Casino's décor resonates with resplendent taste, from its atrium with 28 onyx Ionic columns to its stained glass windows, footbridge and fountains. Guests' dress reflects this sense of style, with jacket and tie required.

La Vigie, usually booked one year in advance, is an exalted example of villa living, mixing an of-the-moment allure with an eminent history and a resounding sense of style.

VILLA MALAKOFF

VILLA CIMA

Villa Malakoff & Villa Cima at Villa d'Este

It has been written that heaven and earth meet on the shores of Lake Como.

Villa Malakoff and Villa Cima are two of the newest private residences opened on the incomparable Villa d'Este estate on Lake Como in Italy. For over 2,000 years, poets like Virgil and Tennyson have found inspiration on its shores.

Villas Malakoff and Cima are situated within a 16th-century 25-acre estate of superbly manicured lawns, mosaic walls and garden paths, next to one of the world's most enchanting bodies of water. The villas, available for short-term tenancies, uphold the patrician atmosphere of the lake region and the aesthetic integrity of Villa d'Este.

Villa Malakoff is a three-story Russian constructivist castle with an intricate play of angles, arched windows and a turreted roof. Its striking sienna exterior stands out among a green wooded landscape and the vast blue water.

Originally built in 1860, Villa Malakoff is a spacious 2,700 square feet of eminent design. It is comprised of a living and dining room, kitchen, and four double-bedded guestrooms, each with en suite dressing rooms and marble baths. Two private terraces face the lake, shielded from the Italian afternoon sun by sloped awnings. Updated with an interior elevator and central air-conditioning, the villa is about 100 meters from the lake shore and the cardinal building.

Cima is a Swiss-style chalet built in 1815 located directly on the lake shore. Its wraparound terrace gives access to stunning water views with a mountainous backdrop. This residence is 7,000 square feet distributed among three floors: the lake, ground and first levels. It has all the amenities of Villa Malakoff but with five bedrooms, each of which faces the lake with large private balconies that take in the grandeur of the countryside.

Accommodations at Villas Malakoff and Cima are memorable for their gentle breezes, cool linen sheets, Como silk and blissful silence. Each room is different in size and décor but contains period furniture, oil paintings and silk accents. Services such as butlers, private chefs, housekeeping, in-villa continental breakfast and chauffeured limousines elevate guests' stay to a level befitting the opulent surroundings.

Dining in this resort is a moveable feast served throughout the day. Italian haute cuisine can be enjoyed on the exclusive veranda with electronically-controlled windows that disappear into the ground—an experience for which jacket and tie are required. Guests can also dine under the shade of a 500-year-old plane tree, on a sundeck overlooking the lake's built-in floating pool or in the terrace bar amidst the scent of jasmine.

Composer Franz Liszt said, "When you write of two happy lovers, let the story be set on the banks of Lake Como." Within the illustrious structures of Villa Malakoff and Villa Cima, many such stories wait to be written.

> *"A lavishly appointed floating retreat moored snugly against the strand of Princess Royal Island, this nature-draped hotel is a sumptuous haven and rejuvenating refuge from all life's cares."*

Remote Hideaways

Whether backpacking across a Chilean rope bridge near Glacier Grey, basking in a Hawaiian spa, sipping champagne above the cliffs of Big Sur, or bear-watching in British Columbia, luxury, anonymity, and escape are key to these exotic destinations.

King Pacific Lodge

In a wilderness setting as pure as the first day of Creation, King Pacific Lodge lies north of Vancouver, British Columbia, gleaming like a polished emerald in Barnard Harbor. A lavishly appointed floating retreat moored snugly against the strand of Princess Royal Island, this nature-draped hotel is a sumptuous haven and rejuvenating refuge from all life's cares.

Accessible only by float-plane, the lodge features both sightseeing and sporting excursions into lush mountains and verdant cedar forests, placid lakes, and the open sea. Led by expert guides, guests can fly-fish and troll for salmon and rainbow trout, kayak and canoe along streams and rivers, hike a wilderness trail, or simply pad about snapping photos in rain forests teeming with flora and fauna. Bear-watching expeditions are also available, as are trips in which multitudes of wildlife including seals, otters, eagles, wolves, and dolphins may be glimpsed. For those wishing a more sweeping view of Nature's northern artistry, helicopter flights over the island are offered.

Aptly named, the King Pacific Lodge exudes a luxuriousness fit for royalty. King-sized beds, overstuffed lounges, handcrafted coffee tables, slate-trimmed bathrooms with expansive ocean views, and private decks are a few of the amenities helping merge guests with their environment. There are pre-bed massages and aromatherapy, as well as a veritable library of good books proliferating throughout.

The culinary excellence of the lodge is as delightful as the King Pacific's beautiful setting. Decorated in an al fresco motif, the dining room is all wood and leather, its oak-and-pine appointments radiating a rustic elegance that serves to sharpen the appetite; here the executive chef creates an array of masterpieces to tempt every palate.

Not surprisingly, seafood is a specialty, the daily catch varying from halibut, topped with a delicious pecan crust, to salmon, poached and delicately seasoned, all garnished with an assortment of freshly picked wild berries. Lemon-drenched lobster and large sea scallops sautéed in white wine are also specialties of the house.

After-dinner activities can include use of a game room with shuffleboard, billiards, and cards. There is a fully-equipped gym, and a Great Room containing a high-powered telescope for star-gazing, which also features a mini-bar serving brandy and cordials for the perfect nightcap.

Whether in search of relaxation, sport, luxury, escape, or simply spectacular views, King Pacific Lodge offers customized trips based on comfort and enjoyment of nature's aesthetics.

Post Ranch Inn

Situated in the Big Sur Mountains on California's towering central coast, an Eden of awe-inspiring land and seascapes, the Post Ranch Inn's singular design allows it to meld harmoniously with the grandeur of its natural surroundings.

Providing the ultimate in privacy and refinement, this cozy mountaintop retreat of 30 bungalows incorporates four distinctive room styles: five Ocean Houses recessed in the side of the ridge, with sloped rooftops covered in native grasses and wildflowers; seven Tree Houses perched on stilts nine feet above the ground, offering a stunning panorama from a window seat surrounding the bed; ten others called Coast Houses and two more known as Mountain Houses, which are cylindrical and named for the views they provide; and six are located in the three-level Butterfly House, which resembles a butterfly with outstretched wings.

All rooms are designed to furnish luxury and comfort to the highest degree. Each has a king-size bed, wood-burning fireplace, indoor spa tub, private terrace, and massage table. Amenities include a wide assortment of coffees and teas, a refrigerator with non-alcoholic beverages and snacks, thick velour robes, slippers, and walking sticks. The rooms also contain a CD stereo system with forty channels of commercial-free, satellite-provided music.

The world-famous Sierra Mar restaurant, where all tables face the sea, is a glass-enclosed aerie high above the pounding surf. Here, Chef Craig Von Foerster focuses on the area's seasonal and regional offerings, fusing California fare with French and Mediterranean influences. He creates a four course, prix fixe dinner menu that changes daily. Craig believes that the difference between good and average food is sometimes a minute detail and that the energy and care for really great food must come from within. The restaurant has received the Wine Spectator's Grand Award yearly since the restaurant's opening in 1992.

The Inn's basking pools overlook the infinite expanse of Pacific blue and are situated to also provide striking views of the surrounding Ventana Mountains. The Post Ranch offers the finest in wellness treatments, including the signature "La Stone Therapy" which relaxes muscles and balances body energy with Big Sur jade. For activity lovers, there is high-tech fitness equipment, nature-trail walks for viewing wildlife such as deer and the magnificent California condor, star gazing through massive telescopes, and herb gardening and yoga classes.

The Post Ranch Inn not only embraces the uniquely romantic and dramatic beauty of Big Sur's coastline, but immerses guests in a luxurious, natural environment.

explora en Atacama

Featuring memorable explorations of remote regions of South America, the Explora Company's objective is promoting new modes of travel and unexplored destinations to those with a passion for discovering exotic locales and unique cultures.

One such place at the crossroads of time combining stunning landscapes, colorful cultures and modern luxury, is Chile's Atacama region, a perfect blend of the historic and the contemporary.

You'll relish the sight of Inca ruins dotting the countryside before a breathtaking backdrop of smoldering volcanoes. Though the region is primarily Spanish-speaking, the ancient Indian languages of Aymaran and Mapudungan are still heard in parts. Located in the high sierra, Atacama stands 8,000 feet above sea level and nearly brushes the heavens.

A few hours are all that is necessary to acclimatize. Explorations on foot or by van as well as horse-riding and climbing tours, are memorable affairs for the terrain boasts some of the world's most impressive scenery: desert and oasis alongside rugged cordilleras, shimmering salt plains, hot bubbling springs, geysers, and rolling hills bisected by clear cool streams. The Atacama sky is filled with radiant sunshine 90% of the year.

Guests arriving at Explora's Hotel de Larache are greeted by eager staff who invites you to sample a pisco sour and to hear details of many different explorations offered by expert guides. Plush accommodations afford the pinnacle of remote luxury, from the private hot springs and massage rooms to the king-size beds and wood armoires. Oversized showers, delicately patterned tiles, and 21st-century conveniences compliment wide picture windows opening on limitless vistas transfer the outer magnificence directly to the inner space.

Private patios are perfect for those who enjoy sipping morning coffee outdoors or lunching al fresco. The restaurant, featuring an elegant international cuisine, serves among its many dishes a delicious ceviche with vine vegetables, fresh shrimp, salmon and scallops, seasoned with cilantro and zest of lemon. Four spectacular swimming pools surround the property.

The San Pedro Atacama's architecture evokes the spirit of local Indian cultures in its sharp angles and strong primary colors. The rooms line up with corridors leading to large patios, and the corridors all meet at the main building like spokes of a wheel.

Atacama is open year round, its climate a standing invitation to visitors. Winter temps vary from lows of 30 degrees Fahrenheit to highs of 72; in summertime (January-March) the range is from 61 to 90 degrees. For the great majority of the year the thermometer remains at a comfortable 75.

One of the most spectacularly beautiful destinations on earth, an Atacama holiday is unforgettable because it is unique in all the world.

explora en Patagonia

Lying one hundred miles north of Antarctica in the Torres del Paine National Park of Chile, the plains, deserts, and highlands of Patagonia contain some of the most breathtaking geography and diverse animal life in the Americas. This quarter million square miles of splendor is both a photographer's delight and a backpacker's nirvana. With a surprisingly temperate climate, its ecosystem, one of the richest on earth, was declared Biosphere's Reserve by UNESCO in 1978.

Providing easy access for exploring the glacial regions of southern South America, the Explora Company greets travelers arriving from Santiago, Chile, at Punta Arenas and ferries them to an exclusive "base camp," the Hotel Salto Chico in the heart of Torres del Paine National Park. Guests can choose from a menu of different explorations within the 598,000-acre park. Expeditions consist of small groups, no more than ten persons per guide, and include all necessary equipment and provisions.

Activities include half-day hikes to the Lake Grey Peninsula, across the Pingo River via hanging rope bridge; treks to Lake Sarmiento to observe colossal, pearl-white calcium formations along the shore; and photo safaris on horseback to the quincho barbecue site where emphasis is on studying the flora and fauna of the region. During winter storms pumas can sometimes be seen descending from snow-capped mountains.

Full-day excursions of 10-11 hours cover terrain rarely glimpsed by human eyes. Hiking to Glacier Grey, guests sight the Southern Ice Field, full of forbidding beauty and magnificent desolation; the Paine Massif and towering Olguin Mountains rearing high above; and ancient icebergs drifting ponderously and majestically in Lake Grey. A picnic lunch is served near the glacier, and, returning by boat across the lake, travelers receive an up close and personal look at the giant glacier walls.

As a base site, the Hotel Salto Chico is both stylish and functional, with all the best gear available for exploring Patagonia. Situated on the tranquil shore of Lake Pehoe, the hotel features 50 rooms which include six large Exploradores suites, thirty-six Cordillera Paine rooms facing the spectacular Macizo del Paine Mountain range, and eight Salto Chico rooms with a superb view of Salto Chico Waterfall. The hotel's interior design blends traditional lenga and cypress woods with handcrafted slate and copper accents, reflecting a millennia-old Indian heritage.

Also reflecting local culture is Salto Chico's cuisine, featuring foods from the soil and rivers of Patagonia, beef and salmon, lentils and crisp garden greens, along with earthy, flavorful wines from Vina Gracia de Chile vineyard.

An Explora Patagonia vacation combines the pleasure of natural exploration in the pristine southern hemisphere with the comfort and relaxation offered by a superb hotel.

Hotel Hâna-Maui and Honua Spa

Bathed in Hawaiian sunshine and caressed by fragrant trade winds, the Hotel Hâna-Maui and Honua Spa offers quietude and a panoramic vision of sky, mountain, and gardens, stretching past a lava-rocked coast down to the turquoise sea. Gracious and secluded, the hotel welcomes those craving privacy. Celebrities arriving are surprised and gratified by the discretion and respect for anonymity shown by the people of Hana: they do not point out or fuss over well-known figures pulling up to the hotel or the general store.

Winding from the village of Kahului through settings seemingly from the brush of Monet, the road to Hana snakes past bamboo forests and waterfalls splashing beside the road, inviting swimmers into its fern-lipped plunge pools. Fruit trees offer up their treasures: mango, guava, and banana. Banks of wild ginger scent the breeze, and vistas open around every bend.

In Hana town, the pastures roll right up to the main street. At the 69-room Hotel Hâna-Maui, there are still 1946-style bungalows, but all have been renovated to achieve a zen-like ambience and understated elegance. Guests move easily from indoors to out, from the teakwood and bamboo of luxury guest rooms, to the Hotel Hâna-Maui's signature feature: the Honua Spa. Located on an acre of manicured grounds, the spa takes advantage of a spectacular view of Hana Bay. Here, guests luxuriate in ultimate nurturing with massage, facials, and body treatments of every stripe, including hot lava stone massage, aromatherapy, reflexology, mud masks, coconut skin scrubs, and traditional Thai massage.

For recreation and play there is horseback riding along the incomparable Hana coast, a daily yoga class, snorkeling, Hawaiian cultural activities, or relaxing at Hamoa Beach, once described by novelist James Michener (author of Hawaii) as "the most perfect crescent beach in the Pacific."

The Ka'uiki dining room features south-sea originals, with dishes such as Kona cold lobster, pan-roasted Kurrabota pork chops with pineapple brown-butter tart tatin, Okinawan spinach and braised bacon glace. The dinner menu changes daily and creates a unique opportunity for guests to sample both traditional and innovative Hawaiian fare. A visit to the Hotel Hâna-Maui allows travelers to experience a slowing of life's frenetic pace in welcome privacy, glimpse landscapes made from the eruption of ocean volcanoes, and enjoy a rejuvenation of both body and spirit in a lush tropical setting.

"*Nature's unlimited wonders unfold as the luxury yacht cruises through Alaska's Inside Passage or along the rugged coastline of Costa Rica.*"

The High Seas

Privately chartered yachts let you set an individually charted course for the most remote and exotic ports of call. And modern luxury liners redefine sea-going luxury. Forget the shuffle board and buffet lines of the 1990s. Think gourmet meals, showpiece staterooms and spas on par with world-class hotels. Sail the high seas in high style, surrounded by creature comforts and some of the most high-tech toys known to man.

MY Revelation

Luxury yacht travel is a juxtaposition of two worlds, affording the most lavish, opulent on-board surroundings to contrast the pristine wilderness that lies beyond. Customized travel routes allow the choice of a low-key cruise or a high-octane get-away—and you decide just how far away from it all you'd like to get.

The 180-foot, 10-12 passenger Revelation is exactly what its name promises. You'll wonder why you've never before followed your own personalized itinerary on the world's most scenic waterways. This type of travel really is a revelation. Nature's unlimited, virtually unseen wonders unfold as the luxury yacht cruises seamlessly through Alaska's Inside Passage (to the tiny coves and inlets few tourists see) or along the rugged coastline of Costa Rica, abundant in wildlife and rich ecosystems.

But these adventures are not simply about sightseeing off starboard side; they're about getting up close and personal with nature, getting involved in the environment—sometimes up to your elbows. (No worries—the on-board Wellness Center massage services will work out any well-earned kinks.)

This gorgeous vessel has everything the world traveler has come to expect from any top, landlocked accommodation. There are five guest staterooms all tastefully designed in rich woods and fine leather, and equipped with every imaginable amenity from individual en suite baths to one's own satellite TV. The Master stateroom has a Jacuzzi that is indispensable at night and an adjoining settee that resembles an Old World tea salon in opulence and ambience.

In addition, there's a Wellness Center and Spa stocked with massage essentials and exercise equipment, a thoughtfully supplied bar, plasma TV and stately fireplace in the main salon, two elegant dining areas, and a Sky bar and spa with windows that put the entire outdoors on display.

To add to the adventure, water sports and recreation equipment are plentifully provided. Paddle single- or double-person kayaks out to an unexplored glacier; use the snorkeling and scuba gear to investigate an underwater reef off Baja; set out in a hard-bottomed Novurania skiff for a close-up of the fauna on the Galapagos. There are also jet skis, sailboats and deep sea fishing gear to immerse you in the natural surroundings!

Perhaps the best on-board amenities—and the last word in luxury—are the personal gourmet chef, who will create culinary triumphs tailored to your tastes and made from the finest local ingredients, and an expert naturalist guide who provides accompaniment and enlightenment about the details of each distinct environment that set it so far apart from the everyday.

MY Absinthe

This luxury yacht really kicks it up a notch! The 201-foot, 12-passenger MY Absinthe has the spacious quarters and impeccable accommodations you'd expect in a yacht of Absinthe's calibre, but its toys are what really set it apart—especially the onboard helicopter. It's the world's only mobile or floating heli-skiing operation that can house its guests in such high style.

This is adventure on a grand scale. The Absinthe is best known for its heli-skiing off the shore of British Columbia in the winter months. In the fall, Absinthe sails for the turquoise waters of Mexico, Panama, and Costa Rica. In fact, the mega-yacht can be Chartered for journeys as far north as Alaska and as far south as Antartica.

To get the adrenaline rushing, grab a kayak or get on a roaring Sea Doo to navigate places that others don't even know exist; do some whale-watching or salt-water fishing; alight in a native Indian village in the unspoiled Northwest or embark on an exploration of giant old-growth forests. The possibilities? Endless. The choice? Yours.

Onboard, the adventure is one for all of the senses to enjoy. From the soothing outdoor Jacuzzi that lets you soak under the stars and the towel warmer that wraps you in luxurious heat (once you eventually emerge) to the state-of-the-art sound system and LCD-screen TVs, the amenities are unbeatable.

The spacious staterooms have an elegant, contemporary décor. But pull yourself away from the comfort of your cabin and take a walk to the wine cellar of the Main Salon…complete with grand piano! Hard to believe you're on a yacht.

The Absinthe carries a crew of 20—including a private chef, naturalist guide and massage therapist—that make the experience unforgettable with their unequalled service. Could there be any better way to see some of nature's most magnificent sights?

SeaDream Yacht Club

Somewhere beyond your dreams is SeaDream Yacht Club, whose slogan—"It's Yachting, Not Cruising"—says it all. SeaDream has won Berlitz's highest honors three years in a row, forcing them to create a new category, "Utterly Exclusive"—a step above luxury class.

SeaDream is relatively new, earning its justifiable popularity in just a short time for its exclusive catering to only 55 couples by a staff almost double that in size. Despite the casual, comfortable and relaxed atmosphere, nothing is overlooked.

The carefree attitude on-board belies an earnest attention to detail. For example, while the gourmet meals are served in open-air, unpretentious spaces, there are over 3,000 bottles of wine from which to choose. Food and drinks are all-inclusive and while you are busy splashing in the waves, the staff will place a surfboard nearby in the water piled high with caviar and champagne. It is a rather indulgent touch amidst a casual setting.

What also sets SeaDream apart is its array of destinations. Sure, the Caribbean is extensively covered and is the perfect place to feel cool ocean spray on the available wave runners or take a leisurely romp on a banana boat. But don't overlook the more recent, exotic South American tours or less-traveled European voyages to the stunning cliffs of Turkey, rich in culture and history, or Croatia's enchanting coastline.

Chartering this entire craft is a great option—the ultimate experience in personalized, precision travel. With the ships' capability to enter even very small ports, you have a world of choices.

Even remaining on-deck feels like a glamorous destination. Designed in teak wood with nautical accents, the yacht boasts a fitness center and spa (the only one in the world exclusively staffed by the Thai Spa Association), a cozy piano bar and casino that let you feel like you've traveled to Monte Carlo even when you're on the other side of the world, fine Belgian linens and Balinese day beds that are so exquisitely comfortable, you may wish to spend the night under skies resplendent with stars. The staff supplies pillows and cozy duvets to counter the chill of fresh ocean air.

While each room onboard is a stylish suite, I recommend the Commodore Club State Room over the Owner Suite. It has his-and-hers bath facilities (stocked with Bulgari personal products) and a private dining area which seats four, perfect for enjoying company.

After a light lunch, make use of the 30-course golf simulator to keep your game up to par without having to hire a caddy. Where else can you play on world-class greens—amidst blue ocean?

SeaDream yachting is the type of travel that puts the world at your fingertips. See where your dreams can take you.

Silversea Cruises

Silversea combines the magnificence of a world-class hotel with the graciousness of a friend's home. This Italian-based cruise line is specifically tailored to the ultra-luxury market, so its ships are spacious yet small compared to mass market vessels—giving them an air of warm intimacy and exclusivity.

Each guest's arrival is marked by a traditional white-glove greeting and a flute of chilled champagne. All-inclusive fares always include an ocean-view suite—80% feature a private, teak veranda—where bowls of fruit are replenished daily, stationery is personalized and a writing desk is provided in your suite sitting area, and canapés are delivered each afternoon. Complimentary beverages are served throughout the ship including a premium assortment of fine wines and spirits. Quite honestly, the service is all-frills, all the time.

Like its worldly clientele-ranging from British royalty and celebrated CEOs to upstart tech wizards and well-heeled doctors—the ships offer an unforced elegance, posh but unpretentious. It is not unusual to see tuxes and evening dresses mingling among more casual resort wear in the Humidor Cigar Lounge or taking in the musical revues and Moonlight Movies.

Each vessel-Silver Cloud, Silver Wind, Silver Shadow, and Silver Whisper-is a grand stage on which to travel to gorgeous settings. World travelers know that access is everything. The ships' intentionally smaller size allow them to slip into remote ports which larger vessels can't navigate, affording passengers unique interactions with locals, unspoiled lands and sights unseen by most tourists.

Follow your dreams around the world and beyond your imagination on Silversea's annual World Cruise across six continents.

Upscale touches have won Silversea accolades from *Travel + Leisure* and other discerning travel publications. The cruise line boards classical musicians at specific ports to entertain its guests, as well as famous chefs, golf experts and speakers for enlightened lectures on local culture. And drawing from its vast Epicurean reserves, Silversea also offers the first wine-themed restaurant at sea. Cuisine is remarkable, in part because of Silversea's collaboration with Relais Chateaux-Relais Gourmands. And Silversea distinguishes itself as a partner with some of the world's most prestigious luxury purveyors, which means every small touch from beauty products to bedding comes with the imprimatur of the world's most honored houses.

Ambassador Isabella Rossellini is not only the face of Silversea, she is also the perfect embodiment of its easy elegance, timeless grace and international glamour.

Crystal Cruises

If individual choice is top priority, the answer is crystal clear. Crystal Cruises has an abundant selection of activities and amenities that distinguishes it from other fleets and allows every passenger to customize their cruise. You may all be in the same boat…but no two travel experiences will be exactly alike.

Want something to e-mail home about? Consider a destination-specific cruise to a penguin colony in Punta Arenas. Or explore the location shooting for Lord of the Rings in a luxurious cruise to lush New Zealand. Crystal offers behind the scenes expeditions into places others overlook completely.

Don't take just a snapshot glimpse of Dubai and reboard. Crystal encourages you to see the inner workings of the city's stables, which house some of the world's finest racehorses, by providing a knowledgeable guide. One of the ship's hand-picked European staff members will lead a tour through historic Canterbury to make the Tales come alive. Had enough of dry land—how about a walk on the ocean floor in Bora Bora? Crystal provides these well-thought out expeditions for world travelers who thought they had seen it all.

On-board options are just as eclectic and exhilarating (with special activities held just for kids). The physically active can choose from Tai Chi classes or dance lessons given by talented instructors. The artistically inclined can take digital photo shops, piano lessons and stone sculpture classes or enjoy film and theater festivals. For the adventurous, shark diving is a once-in-a-lifetime opportunity. And to make it possible to speak with the locals, Berlitz offers beginner language courses on deck.

After feeding your mind, choose from a diverse menu selection for dinner, which is scheduled for two fixed times in the evening to free you up for other pursuits, such as an after-dinner production choreographed by Tony award-winners. Even relaxing in a luxe cabin is enjoyable with ocean views off a magnificent veranda. Highly recommended are the Symphony's and Serenity's Penthouse Suites, which come with full butler service.

On Crystal Cruises, choices are as unlimited as the ocean and each travel experience is exactly as you make it.

Regent Seven Seas Cruises

Convenience is the ultimate luxury. Regent (formerly Radisson) Seven Seas Cruises makes that clear by offering an atmosphere more like that of a private country club than a large cruise liner. Each detail is taken care of and all gratuities and services are included in the initial cost—so guests are free to enjoy their getaway.

Regent sets the standard for all-inclusive, spot-on service: chilled champagne is in your suite upon arrival; fresh flowers are a constant. While passengers are busy seeing the world, staff sees to the smallest details.

The spacious suites display a sense of elegant ease and simplicity, designed in clean lines and bold colors. With top-shelf amenities (including replenishing mini-bars and fruit bowls) and individual balconies, each room is an inviting oasis in the middle of the ocean. Grand and Master Suites are the largest and come with private butler service.

Suites also have walk-in closets—a rarity on most cruise ships but convenient for bringing along your best evening clothes for the ships' formal nights.

Each Regent ship—the smaller Navigator, mid-sized Voyager and larger Mariner—has a limited number of guests, allowing ample opportunities for getting to know fellow passengers and preserving a social club feel. This also maintains an impressive staff-to-guest ratio, ensuring gracious service like a bar staff that remembers your drink order from the first day.

While this service should come with a warning that passengers will become spoiled after a few days at sea, Regent never loses sight of guests' desire for adventure. See the stars from the other side of the equator in the ship's Galileo Observation Lounge as you circumnavigate South America; take your soul someplace new on an eco-excursion with oceanography expert Jean-Michel Cousteau; explore in luxury.

Regent Seven Seas Cruises gives luxury travelers a whole new world to see—and a whole new world of comfort, convenience and style in which to see it.

"*Each first-class seat is actually an individual suite configured for maximum privacy and space.*"

Sleeping Above the Clouds

The world's best airlines have advanced the concept of first class, achieving a higher stratum of comfort, privacy and flying in style. So sink into the soft leather of your fully reclining sleeper seat as you prepare to ascend above the clouds. Fasten your seatbelt...it's going to be a fantastic flight.

Emirates First Class

Emirates First Class is like spending the night in a luxury hotel—in the sky. Each first-class seat on its spacious Airbus, with service from New York to Dubai, is actually an individual suite configured for maximum privacy and space. Only 12 private compartments are available on every flight, all finished in the finest leather and genuine walnut, with such high-shelf amenities as full flat beds, TVs with over 500 channels and revolutionary lighting to help reset body clocks and reduce jet lag.

The flying experience is further personalized as passengers can order their own customized meals at any time during the flight through an Emirates' first—Room Service above the clouds.

It's these incredible details that place Emirates above the rest—and on Forbes' Top Ten List of Airlines. The first-class cabin is attended to by the highest crew-to-passenger ratio of any airline, earning it more than 270 international awards for unsurpassed service and quality cuisine. The lavish on-board atmosphere—with shower facilities, lush greenery and a unique ceiling lighting system that makes stars appear overhead—is supplemented with state-of-the-art technology capabilities and highly-trained, multi-lingual personnel who see to every need.

As an additional service to spoil its passengers on the ground, Emirates offers a complimentary 30-minute massage and use of its exclusive G-Force Health Club between flights or on layovers. Its Marhaba Lounge is open 24 hours and is set up as a majlis, a traditional Arabian rest area that will have passengers wishing for their flight to be delayed—a rare occurrence due to Emirates' impeccable on-time performance. Emirates has added an additional 75 flights per week, which make this airline a major world player.

The Emirates Group has also established a Destination and Leisure Management Division at its headquarters in the vibrant city of Dubai, facilitating travel and leisure activities for its passengers. We use these destination services to orchestrate Arabian adventures for travelers, including safaris on the desert dunes (rich in wildlife) and therapeutic treatments at the Al Maha Desert Resort and Spa.

Emirates makes accommodating passengers its highest priority and covers every conceivable aspect of luxury travel, consistently exceeding expectations in order to satisfy world travelers.

Japan Airlines First Class

When would you wish that a 14-hour flight could actually last longer? When you fly Japan Airlines first or business class from the U.S. to Japan. The JAL staff exemplifies the courtesy, hospitality, splendid service and attention to detail for which the country of Japan is well-known. Additional amenities turn in-flight travel into a transcendent experience.

As might be expected from the technological brilliance of the Japanese, JAL has richly innovated passenger comfort and state-of-the-art cuisine as well as entertainment.

JAL has introduced the sky sleeper solo seat, created by prominent British industrial designer Ross Lovegrove. This elegant seat is an example of "living sculpture" that utilizes natural curves and organic design concepts to produce not only a modern, space-age look with clean lines and sleek styling, but a new level of comfort, luxury, personal space and self-sufficiency.

The First Class cabin holds only 11 of these units, which have a silver exterior shell lined with beige leather from Poltrona Frau, Inc. (recognized for crafting the interiors of luxury cars worldwide) and are outfitted with personal large-screen monitors, viewing glasses, laptop accessories and privacy partitions. The sky sleeper seats recline to a fully flat position, providing a length of over six feet and a width of 2.2 feet, each equipped with a lumbar massage function to alleviate any stress and deliver passengers to their destination refreshed and ready to take on a world of new sights and exquisite culture.

JAL's innovative seating in the Seasons Business Class is part of the airlines' Good Sleep Service, which provides "Do Not Disturb" or "Wake Me for Meals" signs, depending on one's priorities. If reinvigorating rest is first on your list, JAL offers lounge wear and down pillows, as well as sandwiches, snacks or light meals available any time after awakening. Eye refreshers and moisture masks are also provided to make passengers look as fresh as they feel.

However, it is strongly recommended that you don't skip the artistically presented Japanese meals, overseen by the Kyoto Cuisine Mebaekai, a group of new-generation owners of established restaurants serving fine traditional fare, or the succulent Western-style meals prepared by the Association des Disciples d'Auguste Escoffier du Japon, an organization of chefs from top-class Japanese hotels and restaurants specializing in French cuisine.

As part of the Oneworld alliance, JAL is able to expedite travelers' between-flight transfers to other airlines. Superbly-designed Sakura Lounges at domestic and international airports ensure that the time before boarding will be as pleasurable or productive as JAL's remarkable flights of fancy.

Although JAL has embraced cutting-edge technology, the airline has maintained focus on its most important tradition: total passenger satisfaction. Perhaps the kimomo-clad flight attendants have gone, but the traditions of yesterday are clearly visible in JAL's world-renowned level of luxury service and exquisite attention to every detail.

Singapore Airlines First Class

Singapore Airlines has one of the youngest, most advanced fleets in the air. Its service and amenities redefine first-class, with sumptuous and cutting-edge details that ensure unforgettable, unparalleled travel and earned it the number two spot on Forbes' Top Ten List of First-Class Flights—and the number one spot on your travel itinerary.

Singapore Airlines is considered a trendsetter in aviation passenger service, and built a lofty reputation in its infancy when it became the very first airline to offer complimentary headsets and free drinks. Its total customer commitment and meticulous attention to luxury service has garnered the airline a string of awards and accolades, making it the world's most honored airline.

Like the city of Singapore itself, the airline is highly energized and modern. The amenities for passengers range from high-quality toiletries to complimentary writing kits to current reading materials. All of this helps nourish both body and mind to overcome the rigors of travel.

Singapore Airlines perfects the personal touch. The food and wine selection soars to new heights—passengers can choose their meals from expertly crafted dishes prepared by an international panel of chefs and young ones can pick from a fun and brilliant children's menu.

The personalized attention also includes a proper turn-down bed service, a selection of 225 music CDs for a truly individualized listening experience (no iPod needed) and a Premium Services Officer who handles check-in arrangements on the ground while you enjoy the airlines' Silver Kris Lounge, which rivals any L.A. nightspot for sleek design aesthetics.

First-class seating takes the form of Sky Suites—12 exclusive, custom-crafted leather seats housed in a stylish cabin. Business seating is referred to as Raffles Class, the highlight of which is their new Italian-Swiss designed space bed. It allows multiple position options—including a flat sleeping bed—enveloping the travelers in ergonomic comfort. Beds are lined up end to end so that passengers never have to face a seatmate when they seek privacy or uninterrupted sleep.

But the service and cuisine on Singapore Airlines are truly the stuff that dreams are made of—so, tempting as it is, don't sleep through it. Choose a cutting-edge film, order international wine or stroll about the spacious cabin—and experience the art of traveling well.

Exquisite food, cutting-edge design, and comfortable slumber are great innovations. This is an airline that makes the flight one of the best parts of your vacation.

British Airways First Class

No one does proper service like the British—and British Airways FIRST Class is no exception, epitomizing personalized care and attention to detail. It is exemplary service fit for the Queen!

British Airways has been known as the innovator in refined travel since their introduction of FIRST class private pods with six-feet six-inches, lie-flat beds, and they have been continually redefining what travelers have come to expect from world-class flying. This airline set the standards and constantly improves upon them: the latest cushioning technology makes the beds even more restful, as do plumper, full-sized pillows, the best quality fabrics, crisp linens, and luxurious pajamas and soft eye masks that makes for a pampered, perfect sleep.

The service from the specially trained FIRST crew overlooks nothing and includes the most caring, attentive touches, like comforting hot chocolate and cookies before bed and a pre-landing breakfast-in-bed to start visitors off on a smashing holiday.

The FIRST class services ensure that every aspect is attended to—from the pre-flight Molton Brown Travel Spa (complete with the latest treatments and champagne) and stress-free pre-boarding kiosks where passengers can avoid queues and select their own seats in the up-front cabin, to Arrivals Lounges with facilities for post-flight power-showers. British Airways makes travel effortless, allowing passengers to check in online up to one hour before departure then relax in the FIRST Class Airport Lounges, which have the look of Britain's esteemed "exclusive clubs" with warm lighting, soft leather and fully-stocked bars. Pre-flight dinner service is also available in the lounges to ensure uninterrupted sleep on your flight.

To promise an experience of onboard luxury, the airline enlisted leading British interior designer Kelly Hoppen, renowned for her calm, uncluttered style that imparts impressions of both sumptuousness and clean simplicity. Hoppen emulated the opulence of a Rolls Royce interior, employing Connolly leather, burr walnut and plush cashmere finishes in a deep, rich red. The FIRST class demi-cabins are sleek and serene, comfortable and chic, and the sleeper pods boast the last word in luxury and ergonomic design. Even secret agent 007 never had it so good.

These FIRST-class cabins also boast buddy seats, which allow for visits from fellow travelers or family members, to enjoy haute cuisine together in privacy or afternoon tea in a most civilized setting. If passengers choose from the delectable *a' la carte* menu, the FIRST crew prepares the meal exactly to order and serves it at the time request of the passenger.

To add to the experience, each passenger is given a generous supply of high-end personal care products, the likes of which can be found only at the exclusive counters of Harrod's. These are presented in a smart traveling case, a handsome keepsake to remind you of your unparalled flight experience long after your feet have touched the ground.

For attentive service, unsurpassed comfort, and a lovely cup of tea done to perfection, British Airways is the carrier of choice. It is truly a distinguished form of travel.

ACKNOWLEDGEMENTS

My parents, Nancy and Asa Strong, have always supported each of their children (and grandchildren) in all of their endeavors. Through them, we have learned the value of commitment and diligence—and the importance of taking a well-earned vacation! I would like to thank them for their guidance in my life and their assistance with this book, which would never have been completed, or started, without them.

To my wife Kay and my children James, Jennifer and Rodney, I have nothing but enduring love and unbridled appreciation for putting up with me during the long hours that I devoted to this project. They have given me my most treasured memories and a reason to always look forward to returning home after a long flight.

This book could never have been completed without the help of my dedicated and loyal staff, who inspire me with their hard work and keep my appreciation for travel fresh with their enthusiasm. The collective success of Strong Travel Services, Inc. is a testament to them as individuals.

I would like to acknowledge a few of my colleagues for their dedication to the travel industry, their willingness to share their ideas and foresight and, most of all, for their friendship: Matthew Upchurch, Valerie Wilson and her daughters Kimberly and Jennifer, Priscilla Alexander, Peter Bates and Anne Scully. They are all true professionals.

Finally, I'd also like to acknowledge all of the general managers of luxury hotels throughout the world who work ceaselessly to ensure their guests' utmost satisfaction.

They don't just manage superb hotels; they're in the business of bringing dreams to life.